Pat Joe

So Many

Homelands

Berdjouhi
Esmerian

ALSO BY BERDJOUHI ESMERIAN

According to Us
(contributor)

So Many

Homelands

MEMORIES OF A DAUGHTER
OF THE ARMENIAN
DIASPORA

BERDJOUHI ESMERIAN

PICHONE PRESS
ROCHESTER, NY

This book is a memoir. It reflects the author's present
recollections of experiences over time. Some events have
been compressed, and some dialogue has been recreated.

Author photograph by Millie Sigler

Book and cover design by Nina Alvarez of
Dream Your Book - Author Services

For permission to reprint portions of this book, or to order
a review copy, contact: berdjouhiesmerian@gmail.com

ISBN-13: 978-1979079396
ISBN-10: 1979079390

To Eby and Kiki, the preceding generation who started it all, and to Allison, Geoffrey, and Katie (aka KT): the newest generation.

I believe life is too short

for all the worthwhile things

human beings can do.

CONTENTS

Prologue   1
Introduction   2

PART ONE: THE HOMELAND I LEFT BEHIND   5
My Beloved, Beautiful Alex   6
World War II: (A Souvenir of War)   14
The Big *Bombardement*   18
Cairo   22
A Promise To Keep   28
So Many Schools   32
French Cuisine   40
1952-1956   48
Starting College   56
Surviving Beirut   60
One Memorable Day   66
Frog Legs   72

PART TWO: THE HOMELAND I ADOPTED
Why, and How, I Came to the U.S.   78
Thoughts From an Immigrant   84
My First Job in the U.S.   88
The Proofroom, and On   95
A Mother's Day Gift   101
The Stepchild   104
Life With Marcel   109
Once a Week   120
The Story of the CTS (That's a Cadillac, You Know)   124
Twenty-Eight Years Later   127
Diagnosis: Guillain-Barré Syndrome   136
An Experience in the Snow   148
My Best Friend   152
Detachment   156
But Where is the Real *She*?   159
Letter to Eby   166
2017   170

PART THREE: MY ANCESTRAL HOMELAND   175
Finding Armenia   176
And in Conclusion   185
Notes   187
Acknowledgments   189
About the Author   191

PROLOGUE

I am named after my paternal aunt Yester's daughter, who died at the age of two. In Armenian, the name *Berdjouhi* roughly translates to "elegant woman" (or elegant female).

In English, the word elegant originated in the late fifteenth century from Middle French *elegans,* "choice, fine, tasteful," characterized by the collateral form of present participle of *eligere,* "select with care, choose."

Though I was raised in a cosmopolitan city and given a fine education and upbringing, what makes me an "elegant woman" (if indeed that is what I am) is "elegant" in its form *eligere*. I choose everything in this life with care, including the stories collected and fashioned in these pages.

Introduction

Long ago and far away, when I was a child in Alexandria, my parents subscribed us to an Armenian children's magazine called *Pounch*, which means "bouquet" in Armenian, and what a bouquet it was, full of stories and pictures and poems. I loved reading it to my brother, Ohannes. Even today, I am happiest when surrounded by books, be it at a library, bookstore, or running my fingers along the well-populated bookshelves in my home.

Because I love stories, I have always wanted to write.

I had written a short story when I was seventeen. At that time I was attending the German Catholic nuns' school in Alexandria, Egypt. Most of the courses were taught by German nuns, but the language classes—Arabic, English, and French—were taught by lay teachers. Our English teacher was a young White Russian ("White Russian" is an archaism for the eastern part of present-day Belarus) who had received her education in England. I was very fond of her, especially because she taught my favorite language. I asked her one day if she would help me in revising a story. She naturally agreed. It was a very simplistic romantic plot with the heroine as a pretty, but short, girl.

In 1997 or '98 I was pondering the subject of dreams and going through some old papers when I came across the following, written around 1970:

> I hadn't given it much thought. I only knew I wanted it. Now, the textbooks are here and I have to send in my first assignment. Why do I want to become a writer? What do I expect from it? English is not my mother tongue. I learned it when I was very young, partly in school and to a great extent by reading books and magazines in English. But most of all, because I loved it! One of my objectives is to learn more about the English language. This will help me in my correspondence and my conversation.

> A second reason is to learn to organize my thoughts in a presentable manner and make them acceptable to the writing market. I would like to write articles for magazines about today's issues such as politics, war, women's liberation, and above all about life as I see it. My feelings, thoughts, reactions are very real to me. I want to be able to put them down on paper and communicate them to people.

> Since I signed up for the writing course, I've started to teach English to non-English-speaking immigrants in night school. The challenge is marvelous. Twice a week I face my class of grown-ups, most of whom, other than not knowing any English, haven't had much schooling in their own tongue. Some of them do not know the alphabet even in their own language. Twice a week I go through emotions that range from despair to joy that comes from seeing one little progress.

> These experiences have touched me in such a way that I now see the possibility of writing about these and other experiences. In what form this writing will be I cannot say. A series of articles?

Short stories? Or a short novel in time? As my skills in writing develop, I hope I can turn different phases of my life into a permanent record.

I believe life is too short for all the worthwhile things human beings can do.

And I was right. Life *is* too short for all the worthwhile things a human can do. Despite my best intentions, I never became a writer. I made my career running editorial departments of a law book publishing company instead. It wasn't until my sixties—after I retired—that I decided, regardless of how good or bad my writing was, that I needed to try and leave a permanent record of my experiences.

What I tell within these pages is how I perceived and felt events as they were taking place, and how history influenced the choices I had to make in my life. All content relating to world historical events is from my memory.

PART ONE

THE
HOMELAND
I LEFT
BEHIND

My Beloved, Beautiful Alex

Alexandria, Egypt, was built around 331 BC by Alexander the Great along the southern shore of the Mediterranean Sea. Home of the famous Library of Alexandria (one of the seven wonders of the ancient world), Alexandria was still a cosmopolitan city in my day. Two- to seven-story apartment buildings teemed with Greek, Lebanese, Syrian, British, French, Jewish, Italian, Maltese, German, and Armenian people.

Even though everyone spoke Arabic, the official language of the country, all the non-Arab groups kept their own customs and communicated with the neighbors in French, which was also spoken at the banks, department stores, and private boutiques. We grew up speaking each other's languages, learned while playing with neighborhood children and in the schools, but at home we each spoke our mother tongues. For me that language was Armenian.

Most apartment buildings had commercial stores on the street level. These businesses could be groceries, haberdasheries, bakeries, fruit stores, bicycle rentals, hairdressers, barbers, and even small or large pastry shops. And I should not forget the dairies that sold yogurt and ice cream. The stores' names were written in Latin, Greek, or Armenian characters, sometimes also Arabic. The buses and tramways bore Latin and Arabic lettering and numbering.

The Armenians have a very long history in Egypt. A reasonably influential community had sprung up, which included Nubar Pasha, the first Prime Minister of Egypt in the late 1800s, whose statue was placed in a prominent square. During my day, there were some forty thousand of us between Cairo and Alexandria. Some, who were called "the old timers," had settled in Egypt since before the many uprisings in Turkish Armenia during the late 1890s.

Most however were either survivors of the Armenian Genocide of 1915 (also known as the Armenian Holocaust, the systematic extermination of the Armenian population from its historic homeland in Asia Minor by the Ottoman government), or their children.

My father's family had left Turkey around 1910. His older brother, Mguerdich, immigrated to the United States in 1912. Ten years later he had gone to visit his family in Alexandria and during his trip back to his home in the United States the ship stopped in Turkey. He debarked to visit relatives. The massacres started shortly after and the ship would not allow him back on board, because he was considered a Turkish citizen upon the soil where he was born. He was killed in Turkey during the

Smyrna massacres of Greeks and Armenians in 1922. I never knew him.

As for my mother's parents, they had left Armenia a lot earlier and actually met and got married in Alexandria. My mother and her siblings had been born there.

Egypt proved itself a very good host to the genocide survivor refugees who, having found peace, in their turn contributed to the prosperity of their new country. They established schools and cultural centers, built churches, and became welcome and productive citizens. Armenians shone in businesses that required the artistry of their hands. Your shoemaker, shirt maker, tailor, jeweler, watchmaker, photographer, and baker might all be Armenian. There were also prominent professionals such as doctors, architects, and pharmacists, as well as quite a few manufacturers who owned factories and provided employment.

Public transportation was good in Alexandria. Most people had no cars and used the bus or the tramway. Some families owned one car and very, very few had more than one. It is interesting how some identifying names or numbers stay in memory no matter how many years have gone by (even though a lot of day-to-day happenings are forgotten). Our favorite bus was Number 24. It took us downtown for shopping or to the dentist and the Victoria Bookstore and Stationery, located on the street level of the dentist's office.

Going to the dentist was a treat. Yes, a treat. He occupied

the whole fourth floor of a building with architecture common to the European cities of the late nineteenth or early twentieth century. The floors were covered with the largest Persian rugs you can imagine. Oh, the marble games we have played there on those rugs, my brother Ohannes and I!

As you entered the apartment, there were two large waiting rooms. To the left was the office area with the secretary's desk and two adjoining examining rooms so the dentist could go easily from one patient to the next as needed. He often appeared in a jolly manner, almost skipping, with a tune in his voice. He asked me questions, admired my bracelet, and most of all was very, very gentle, even when he had to use the drill.

To the right of the waiting rooms was another very large room with plate glass on the doors through which we could hear canaries singing. When there were no other patients in the waiting rooms, Dr. Kayarian would take Ohannes and me to that room to see hundreds of canaries, both yellow and white, in large cages along the four walls. We watched and inspected the various species while Dr. Kayarian changed their water or refilled their feeding boxes.

As we left the dentist's office, we invariably stopped at the Victoria Bookstore to search for the latest issues of comic magazines. We loved to read *Superman, Spiderman,* and my favorite, *Captain Marvel.* We also bought British comics called *Film Fun* featuring both British and American comedians like

Laurel and Hardy, and many others whose names I no longer remember. Mother bought her magazines: *Woman and Home, Woman's Own, Woman's Home Companion.* I loved to browse through the books, greeting cards, and anything one can find in such a store full of treasures.

Summers in Alexandria were hot and humid, perfect weather for the beach, and every year we followed a specific ritual. Schools were out after the first week in July until the first week in October. We went to the beaches in the daytime and, at least twice a week, to the movies in the late afternoon or evening. Movies lasted about two-and-a-half hours then: the newsreel, a cartoon, sometimes a documentary, and the trailer for the following week's feature film, ending with a fifteen-minute intermission. During intermission we would buy ice cream called *klo-klo* from the concession vendors who went up and down the aisles with their trays full of refreshments. After that we watched the feature film, usually an American Western, musical, or comedy approved by Father—no romantic stories for us kids. We also saw Egyptian, English, French, and Italian films. We grew familiar with the film stars of all these countries.

At other times we went to the *patisseries* with French and Greek names such as Athineos, Beaudrot, Delices, Groppi, Tornazaki, Trianon. We would each select two pieces of pastry and a cup of coffee or tea. The pastries were much smaller than the ones we have here. Two *éclairs*, or one *éclair* and one *mille-*

feuilles (Napoleon) amounted to even less than the size of just one *éclair* here.

Some of these *patisseries* were set on the Corniche along the seashore. This was a wide street along the Mediterranean and a favorite route for Sunday drives. The Egyptian gardeners came in the evening to sell necklaces strung with jasmine flower buds, which would open up as the evening went on, and our necks gave off the scent of jasmine. The tramway stations had names like Sporting, Camp de Cesar, Ibrahimieh, Cleopatra, Glymenopoulos, Stanley Bay, Victoria, Baccos, and Sidi Bishr One, Sidi Bishr Two, and Sidi Bishr Three. Did you notice the various languages? Beyond the three Sidi Bishrs came Mandara and then Montazah, where King Farouk had his summer palace. These stops led to the whitest and smoothest sandy beaches.

King Farouk owned large guava orchards on the grounds of Montazah Palace. The orchards were open to the public during his reign and we could go there, pick and eat as many guavas as we wanted, and on the way out pay for what we took home with us. This was a favorite Sunday afternoon outing during guava season. Father often said that Farouk could have gained more support from his citizens if he had given all the fruit to his subjects instead of charging them, especially since he really did not need the money.

One of our favorite beaches was Stanley Bay. There were four stories of cabins built in a crescent shape along the back edge of the beach with the big and small swimming basins; children were allowed only in the small one. The small basin's boundaries were enclosed with large rocks, the waves minimal, and the water not too deep. The big basin was open to the sea. Here one could swim as far as one wanted, keeping the lifeguards on constant alert.

After we came out of the water, we would either have sandwiches from home, or better yet, go to the falafel restaurant. It was more like a booth, really, and had only take-out—it resided on the west side of the hotel behind the cabins. The owners were two Greek brothers—one slim and one round—who reminded me of Laurel and Hardy. In their short-sleeved shirts and white aprons, they stood behind the counter and sold the most delicious falafel in the world. One did the cooking, the other prepared the flat, five-inch pita sandwiches filled with shredded lettuce, about four or five flat falafel balls, and a few slices of cucumber pickles. Those sandwiches were the best part of these outings as far as I was concerned.

Recreational alcoholic drinks in Egypt were beer and scotch. People also served liqueurs during afternoon or evening visits, accompanied by a spoonful of a homemade jam of dates, apricots, rolled-up bitter orange peel, figs, or some other fruit. The beer factory in Alexandria, which brewed Stella, was on the same street where I was born. I often joke that the first scent I smelled as a newborn was that yeasty aroma, and that is why I love beer.

Alexandria was my birthplace and my home until the age of twenty-nine. After coming to the United States, I never went back. Maybe it's just as well; no place remains the same after so many years. I can keep my memories intact in which the life, colors, scenery, and even smells that surrounded me are revived, the years in between melt away, and I am transported back to the Alexandria of my youth.

Even the years of the Second World War, which began when I was only a child, are revived.

World War II: (A Souvenir of War)

I was six years old when World War II started in the fall of 1939.

I still remember how my parents hung black curtains on the windows to keep the lights at night from showing outside. They also glued strips of tan-colored paper to the windowpanes in a diamond pattern. It was supposed to minimize the spray of shattered glass. They bought flashlights and painted a blue ring around the front glass covering to minimize the amount of light when we had to go outside at night. All the cars had the same blue ring painted around their headlights. I remember that when the war ended on May 8, 1945, and the blackout was lifted, my father took Ohannes and me to the main street near our home so we could see the streets finally lit up at night—we were too young to remember the "good old days" of streetlights.

I took every new experience with the innocence of childhood. In general the war did not frighten me except for the gas masks all British subjects were given. These horrid things were worn over the whole head, had round, bulging eyepieces, and a long hose (to supply oxygen) from the mouth area to the box hanging from the shoulder. It just did not look natural; to me it was a monster. Our family did not have any of these, because we were Egyptian subjects, but our upstairs neighbors, a Maltese family, did. The Maltese were British subjects. The husband was a volunteer warden, which meant that during air raids he had to patrol the streets in his uniform and carry his gas mask. His wife was of Jewish descent. As time went on, it was feared that the husband might have to go into the British Army and his wife and daughter might end up in a concentration camp. My father reassured them that he would keep them with us and take care of them. But it never came to that; the family eventually immigrated to Australia and we lost touch with each other.

Alexandria had its share of air raids, bombs, damaged houses, and casualties. To this day, whenever I hear fireworks but do not see them, a strange feeling starts in my chest and I think of anti-aircraft guns. It is irrational, I know, but it is a souvenir of war for me and many others.

The presence of British ships in the Mediterranean Sea was important to the Allies. Alexandria, a port city and a protectorate of Britain, was the logical place to dock war ships. This in turn made us also a target for bombardments just like most European cities Germany was attacking.

On many nights we had air raids, sometimes more than once a night. The apartment building across from our house had a well-planned shelter and it was fun for us children to wake in the middle of the night, go to the shelter, and play with friends who had also come there with their parents. We learned to differentiate the sound of the Allied airplanes from that of the German planes. The latter had a drone, while the British planes had a smoother sound. We got used to hearing the whistling of the bombs as they fell, and then the explosion, as our parents tried to identify the location that got hit.

For many years people talked of the miraculous church in the city's downtown area. One night two bombs fell, one on each side of it, leaving the church unharmed.

Mother had our rush to the shelter organized like a science. When we went to bed, she would fold our clothes and set them in a pile in the order we would be wearing them, next to our beds. As soon as the sirens started, she and Father would dress us, wrap us in big triangular crocheted shawls, tie them at the back, and carry us across the street and into the shelter.

Everyone was not as safety conscious as our parents. My mother's parents, Néné and Dédé, and her sister, who was only eleven years older than I was (we called her Vartoug like the grown-ups), often spent the night at our home. On nights with a full moon we could expect severe bombardments, but Dédé and Vartoug refused to go to the shelter every time. My grandfather would turn the lights off, pull the curtains open, and watch the "fireworks" as he called them. Vartoug's excuse was that she'd have to go to school in the morning, so she needed to sleep.

Indeed, in spite of the war, life continued with all normal activities: work, school, shopping, movies, and going to the beach, though it was not unusual to see military personnel from different Allied countries in the streets and restaurants.

One time we had gone to the restaurant at the beach called Palais. A group of British soldiers were there and one of them was playing on his accordion. They were encouraging the patrons to request songs. Someone in our group decided to ask for a song. I was told to go and give the title of the song to the soldier. Even though I did not know any English at the time, it was not difficult to repeat the name. So I approached the accordion player and gave him the request. One of the other soldiers in the group picked me up and put me on his knees and hugged me until the song was over and then let me go. I've never forgotten the expression in his face. Did I remind him of a daughter he had left behind? Or perhaps a little sister? Did he ever get back safe and unharmed and hug his little girl again?

Gradually the war grew more intense and families started moving south to the smaller towns and villages. My parents decided to stay in Alexandria until one night in April of 1941 when everything changed.

THE BIG BOMBARDEMENT

One unforgettable night, when the air raid sirens started, my parents went through their usual routine of getting us dressed and rushing to the shelter across the street. In order to get her sister to go also, Mother told Vartoug she needed her to carry the thermos bottle. Reluctantly Vartoug agreed. Néné came along too, but nothing would budge my Dédé from his routine. "My mother's blessing is still with me and is strong enough. It will protect me," he said. The bombardments were getting heavy and fierce. We had been in the shelter hardly ten minutes when we heard the familiar whistling of a falling bomb, and soon thereafter the big explosion. Just as always, when the whistling sound of the falling bomb started, everyone tried to identify the location it hit. Well, this time, there was no need to guess: we knew it was very, very close.

People from the neighborhood started rushing into the shelter and pretty soon the place got packed with maybe over one hundred people. Soon there was no room to sit—just stand very, very close. At first I could only see skirts and pants legs, but my parents picked Ohannes and me up, holding us high so we could breathe better. I can still see the faces of my neighbors, bloody, hair blown in all directions turned white from dust. Many were wounded, disoriented, and terribly frightened.

It turned out that the bomb was a torpedo—yes, a torpedo on land—dropped with a parachute aimed at the Alexandria airport not far from our home. The wind drifted the parachute enough to bring it close to a populated section. It fell in the middle of a wide-open space and demolished all the houses in the vicinity.

Our house was one of them—with Dédé in it .

As people came into the shelter, Mother and Néné kept asking them about the exact location of the explosion. Someone told them that the bomb had hit our house. We all thought that Dédé must have been killed and Néné and Mother started crying.

As soon as the air raid was over, Father and Néné ran out to verify the location of the explosion and came back to let us know that somehow our house was still standing.

Dédé was okay.

This is the story he later told: He had just turned the lights off and was getting ready to pull the drapes open to watch the "fireworks" when suddenly all the windows, with shutters closed, imploded. The house was lit up again from the lights of the anti-aircraft guns and search light in the sky. What saved him was the fact that he was out of his bed and standing at the light switch in front of a solid wall. Had he been in his bed, which was right in front of the window, he would most certainly have been injured, maybe killed. His mother's blessing, indeed.

It was a very long night. After the air raid was over, we could not go home. Instead, my father's best friend, who lived not too far, but far enough to have escaped the damage of the torpedo, came to search for us and took us to his home. He was married to a cousin of Mother's and they also had two children. Our two families were very close and spent many evenings visiting together. We stayed there for a few days then Father decided that it was finally time to leave Alexandria for safer grounds.

From then on everyone in the family and the neighborhood referred to this event as "the night of the big *bombardement*," using the French word regardless of what language we were talking. Using French and Arabic words in our conversations was not unusual.

I still remember the small car in which ten of us, all members of related families, were piled up, women and children. One of the men drove us to Cairo, where the war had not reached yet.

From this destruction and upheaval came the happiest year of my childhood: the one we lived in Cairo.

My grandparents did not accompany us at this time. Néné remained to help Father figure out what household and personal items were salvageable and to arrange for transporting them to our new home in Cairo as soon as one had been rented.

I used to take Lisette, my doll, to the shelter during air raids. This particular night I forgot her at home. I told Néné where I kept her and asked her to get her for me. It probably seemed hopeless, but she said yes, she'd try.

We lost almost everything breakable, including all of Mother's china and decorative items. All our toys were destroyed, but Néné found my doll, still tucked away in her special place: a nook next to the big couch.

So, my darling doll Lisette, always dressed in the same knitted outfit as me, went to Cairo with me.

CAIRO

When we arrived in Cairo, we first stayed with friends until my parents could find a house large enough to hold all of us: Néné, Dédé, Vartoug, Uncle Garo, who lived in Cairo already, and our own family. We also needed room for my mother's younger brother, Hagop, who was serving in the Egyptian army and came to stay with us when on leave.

My parents rented an apartment in one of the suburbs of Cairo called Matarieh. According to legend, it is where the Holy Family (Jesus, Mary, and Joseph) lived when they went to Egypt.

The landlord and his wife lived on the first floor, and spiral stairs led to our second-floor apartment. There were ten rooms, a sunroom, and a couple of balconies. One of the balconies was very large and overlooked the garden, twice the size of the building, filled with beautiful and exotic flowers, mango trees that reached our balconies, a swing, and a water well. A jasmine vine grew up the wall to the large balcony. One of the mango trees reached the smaller balcony and we were allowed to pick the fruits as far as we could reach them.

The landlord owned a Dalmatian, which became very fond of us children and would wag its tail whenever it was near us. The wagging of the tail was not welcome by us, because the stiff, thin tail was as hard as a metal pipe, and it hurt when Nip was too close and it hit us.

We spent many happy hours in that garden.

Even though Dédé had had his own business in Alexandria, he gave up working shortly after the move to Cairo. His health was not so good anymore. The big bombardement had had its toll on him. He aged suddenly. However, he was our dear grandfather and kept us always busy with stories of the mischievous little boy he had been. How I wish I could remember those stories.

In Cairo we started piano lessons, attended Nubarian Armenian School in Heliopolis (another suburb of Cairo), had the whooping cough, and had Santa Claus come to deliver us new toys on New Year's Eve.

Christmas is celebrated on January 6 in the Armenian Church. New Year's Eve is a holiday when the Christmas fasting period starts with specially prepared dishes. It is called *Gaghant*. And that is the day Santa Claus *(Gaghant Baba)* comes with presents for everyone but mostly the children. Why do I remember this particular Gaghant? Because, as a big-girl eight-year-old I discovered that there is no Gaghant Baba. It is just a grown-up dressed in the traditional red coat and hat. I saw how Eby Mama and Vartoug would come home after a day of shopping in the city with bags of items they hid in the closet. At one point I saw some of the toys as they removed then from the paper packages. It was not hard to put two and two together.

On New Year's Eve, one of them placed the packages outside our door and came back in quickly after ringing the doorbell. Very innocently, Vartoug opened the door and, "Oh, look at all these. Gaghant Baba was here." Six-year-old Ohannes said, "I don't believe it was Gaghant Baba. It was Vartoug who rang the doorbell." At this point, I, the big sister who knew things he didn't, convinced him with, "Oh yes, it was Gaghant Baba. I saw the edge of his red coat as he was running down the stairs." And I remember being sad that Gaghant Baba was not real.

That was the year Ohannes started composing his music. He had shown a talent for the piano from the age of two by playing, with one finger, any tune he heard on my toy pianos. The toys were mine but he was the one to make music on them. I just played on the white and black sticks as I thought of them. Mother used to play on her own piano, which used to be always locked so the children would not just bang on it. One day, Mother asked Ohannes if he wanted to try the big piano. "Yes," he said. And from that day on Mother's piano was never locked. That year in Cairo he composed a piece he called *The Train*. We lived close to the train line and used to take the ride every time we went to the city. When Ohannes played his piece, you could hear the engines starting up and then the whistle blowing and

1942. Ready for school in front of the jasmine vine on the large verandah.

then the chug-chug of the ride itself. Another piece was called *The Sirens*. It sounded just like the air raid sirens we had become used to, and the whistling bombs falling. Since he didn't know how to write music, Mother would sit with him at the piano and write what he played on music sheets.

Another happy memory of that year is our landlady. She was a wonderful woman and loved us very much. Ohannes developed a special fondness for her. Even though she had three stepsons, she herself had never had children. She had two nieces, who visited her often and sometimes one of them would take Ohannes and me for a walk. We would go up and down the street marching like different soldiers. "Now we walk like the English," she'd say, and we would march a certain way. "Now we walk like the Germans," and up would go each leg with each step, and so on.

Once she took us to a garden and showed us a very big tree with a huge trunk on which there was the silhouette of a woman sitting and leaning on the trunk. According to the inhabitants, it was where the Virgin Mary had sat down to rest and her shadow had created the silhouette.

The landlady dreamed of owning a Packard automobile some day. When we asked her, "What will you wear when riding in your Packard?" she would go to her bedroom and return dressed up in a heavy silk robe, a stylish hat, and smoking a cigarette in a long holder. It was a show for my brother and me.

Whenever she saw something that pleased her extremely well, it would touch her so much that she would faint. But she would never faint and fall on the floor. She would turn around and around and, finding a chair or sofa, fall back onto it. You should have seen us laughing with tears running down our cheeks.

1942. IN THE GARDEN OF THE MATARIEH HOME.
Left to right: Vartoug, Aunt Takouhi, Nene, Mrs. Cherakian, the landlady, Mother. Nip the Dalmatian between Ohannes and me.

A Promise To Keep

About a year later, our happy and peaceful childhood came to an end, not because the war came to Cairo, but because we went back to the war.

Father owned a tool-and-die workshop in Alexandria. My cousin Ashod, Aunt Yester's son, worked for him, as well as a few other employees. One of his work contracts was the Alexandria Water Company. In later years, I loved to go to his workshop, receive a big smile from Ashod, and listen to the machines and the metal pipes falling onto the piles.

Father would often go to the water plants and had seen how the Nile water we used in our homes underwent the many processes to be purified. Whenever he saw water faucets running for no reason he'd tell us, "If you only knew what it takes to clean this water, you'd never waste a drop of it." I guess that's why I also am very careful, even now, not to waste the clean water that flows through our homes, and which we take for granted.

While the family settled in Matarieh and we were enjoying that idyllic year of our childhood, Father did not stay with us full time. In addition to his workshop in Alexandria, he opened another one in Cairo and started weekly trips between the two cities trying to keep both places working. He said he had promised the British owners of the Alexandria Water Company that throughout the war he would supply them with whatever they needed in the line of nuts, bolts, pipes, faucets, etc. Every Monday he drove to Alexandria, attended to his business there, then returned on Friday morning to attend to the business in Cairo.

One Monday, after he had gone to Alexandria as usual, he returned to Cairo in the evening and told Mother, "Pack whatever necessities you will need in some suitcases. We are returning to Alexandria."

As soon as he had arrived in Alexandria that morning, he learned that Rommel and his army were in North Africa marching toward Egypt and would be in Alexandria very soon. He drove right back to Cairo because he was faced with a major dilemma.

The business in Cairo was doing very well, even better than the one in Alexandria. But Father was a man of his word. He knew that if the Germans occupied Alexandria, the route between the two major cities would be closed. If he decided to keep his family in Cairo, he would have to stay with us, and then he would be cut off from his workshop in Alexandria. But he had a promise to keep. So, he solved his dilemma by bringing us back to our Alex.

By now Cairo was also having air raids and blackouts. In the middle of the night, by the illumination of a full moon and searchlights, Mother packed a few clothes, and the next morning we started off.

Father decided to take the village route instead of the faster desert road because it was safer. We had to cross many bridges along the Nile, which is the longest river in Africa. Before each bridge, he'd say, "Just hope they haven't blown this one up." We feared that if the Egyptians had blown up the bridges along the Nile, about seven of them, to prevent the Germans from reaching Cairo, we'd be stranded. But every bridge was yet unharmed, and we continued.

We were not the only travelers on the road, but we were the only ones going northward to Alexandria. The British army and many private citizens were evacuating the city and everyone was traveling in the opposite direction. There were trucks piled high with household items, and cars full of people on their way to the safety of Cairo. People were waving to us to turn around. But we continued.

We went to our renovated home, and as it turned out, after a few days Rommel was defeated and pushed back. Father continued working with the British Water Company and supplied them with the water pipe parts they needed.

Father asked Uncle Garo to run the Cairo branch, but Garo

refused because he didn't know the tool-and-die business. Father closed that branch and we remained in Alexandria. He had a promise to keep.

Years later, Mother often wondered what would have happened if we had not returned to Alexandria, or if her brother had accepted the offer to run the workshop in Cairo. Certainly Father would have been far better off financially. But she always told the story with pride that Father was a man of his word. He had kept his promise.

So Many Schools

In Egypt most children started kindergarten at the age of four (sometimes even three) but my parents considered that too young. They wanted to wait until I was five. They were extremely protective and my small stature did not help the situation.

Finally, in July of 1938, as I turned five, I was registered at the secular German school and started kindergarten in the fall. There was a parochial German school also, run by nuns, but my parents as well as some other Armenian parents preferred the secular school. From the start, Father was planning our future education in Germany. His oldest sister, Yester (Esther), had been at a German school in Turkish Armenia before the family's move to Egypt. Unfortunately, in those days higher education was not considered the proper goal for girls, and my grandmother whom we called Hamama had declined the opportunity for Yester to go to Germany and study further. Instead, Yester got married off to a hearing impaired gentleman and a few years later died at the age of twenty-five, leaving behind her husband and a seven-year-old son, Ashod (who was

1939. Waiting for the school bus.

one of my favorite cousins). I never met her.

This German kindergarten was a new kind of school compared to the usual kindergarten of the time. We did not have typical classrooms with desks and benches, blackboards, and formal lessons. Instead, we had small tables and chairs, and a lot of our activities were like the typical kindergarten activities of schools in the US: playing in the sandbox, taking naps, having our snacks and lunch at the table. We even celebrated each child's birthday with a cake and candles. And, most importantly, we loved our two teachers. There was a third one also, but she was mean and I don't even remember her name.

As this was a German school, we spoke only German and I learned it fluently. The school bus picked me up in the morning, with Schwester Bertha as our teacher escort. I wore my blue uniform, my blue hat with the German flag colors around the brim, and carried my small bag containing a sandwich and fruit.

After a full day of school activities, the school bus returned me home in the early afternoon, this time with Tante Irene as the teacher escort.

But I grew up during a time when world events often interfered with our dreams and their realizations. World War II started in the fall of 1939 and the German school closed down, its personnel returning to Germany. Now my parents had to find a new school for both Ohannes and me. We were enrolled in the kindergarten of the Armenian school Haigaznian

Varjaran (Haigaznian School) established by Father Haigazoon, an Armenian priest. He was the headmaster, and of his five children, two were old enough to teach in the school and three attended the various classes according to their ages.

In the Armenian system (at least at that time) kindergarten classes were named by the various stages of a flower. The first year was called *poghpotch* (small bud), the second year was *gogon* (bud), and the third year *dzaghig* (flower). Children weren't kindergarteners, they were either a poghpotch, a gogon, or a dzaghig.

I became a gogon and Ohannes, now four, was a poghpotch. The following year I became a dzaghig. The best part of dzaghig class was the teacher, Miss Herminée. Of all the teachers I have had in my lifetime, she was the one I loved the most. I used to daydream that someday my Uncle Garo would marry her, and then she would become my aunt.

In the meantime, as the war was intensifying, my parents started talking about keeping us at home and having a teacher come to give us private lessons, similar to homeschooling. This way we would not be at school when air raids started. They thought this would be safer. Panic filled my heart. No school?!

One day I noticed that there were some workers on the playground, digging for who-knows-what reason, and I came up with a plan. At home that evening I announced to my parents that Father Haigazoon was building an underground shelter for classes and would be moving all the desks there so that the students would be safe during the day. My parents never dreamed this was the fabrication of a wild imagination. It didn't work, but it was worth the try.

Even though we didn't get to stay in our beloved school, something wonderful happened. Miss Herminée came to our home three times a week and taught us our lessons. But this didn't last long either, and after the Big Bombardement, we went to Cairo and started classes at Noubarian Armenian School in Heliopolis, a very nice suburb, for the school year 1941–1942. Even though this was another happy experience during a very happy year of our childhood, that's all it was, only one year. This time I was past kindergarten and was placed in the special preparatory class before elementary school. I again found another wonderful teacher, Miss Archaluyse (which means "dawn " in Armenian).

Many years later, in 1962, the Kaloustian National School of Cairo had organized a trip to Upper Egypt to visit the ancient ruins during the school break at Eastertime. Mother, Uncle Garo, and his wife, Aunt Zabel (no, he didn't marry Miss Herminée) came along. To my surprise and delight, Miss Archaluyse joined the expedition and when I introduced myself to her, she remembered me.

After our happy year in Cairo, we returned to Alexandria and to Father Haigazoon's school. Then father decided to send us to the Boghosian National Armenian School of Alexandria instead, where we spent four years.

The private schools of the various nationalities taught all subjects in the language of the school. In addition, every school taught Arabic, French, and English as foreign languages. We all took every single class given—no electives. My best subjects were French and English. I was a good student, but that doesn't mean I always behaved.

Once in a while, the devil inside me would make itself visible. About three years into Boghosian, we had been given a poem to memorize for English class. It was a pretty long one. I had no problem with it, and had done my homework, but most of the rest of the class had been having difficulties with it. I decided to help them. I told them that the teacher was an Englishwoman and she did not know any Armenian. I wrote the whole poem in Armenian letters on the blackboard and all they had to do was read it. We would tell the teacher that the Armenian teacher had asked us not to erase this special assignment for the next class.

Our headmaster had the habit of strolling the hallways and here and there opening a classroom door and entering just to make his presence known or just to make sure all was well. While our class was in progress, the door opened suddenly and we saw his head peek in and just look around. *Hold your breath!* Then he closed the door. *Sigh of relief.* The door opened again and he walked in and looked at the blackboard.

We were in trouble .

The headmaster wanted to know who wrote this. No one owned it up; my classmates protected me. Since there was no culprit to punish, all we got was a reprimand and more visits from the headmaster during future classes.

The war ended in May 1945. For years, Mother had been trying to persuade Father that we needed to be in non-Armenian schools to learn English more proficiently. Finally, at the end of the school year 1946–1947 Ohannes was registered at British Boys' School and I at Deutche Schule der Borromäerinnen (German School of the Borromeo Nuns). During the summer vacation months, I went to the new school three times a week to take private lessons in German to be able to follow classes when the school opened.

Changing schools almost yearly was one of the hardest things for Ohannes and me. Some were happy years, others were tolerable, but the hardest was leaving friends we had made and having to make new ones all over again. But I stayed at Deutche Schule der Borromäerinnen for five years, until graduation.

I remember asking Mother Superior, Mutter Angelika, for advice as to how and where in Germany I could apply for a university, but she discouraged my parents from sending me. "Germany is not a good place at the moment to send a young girl on her own," was her answer. And the answer to that was for me to attend an English school to perfect my English so that I could now go to England instead. Many students who had attended their own schools used to go to either an English or a French school for two to three years to improve their languages so they could work as secretaries in private offices or at the banks—the "proper" jobs for young girls.

My plans were different. I wanted to go to England or to the United States to study medicine .

I started at the Scottish School for Girls where many of my classmates were Armenians and Greeks and Lebanese who had first been to their own schools like me. My mother had attended the same school and my English teacher was the same one who had taught her. Miss Meliné Atanassian. She was Armenian.

I will never forget Miss Meliné. She was very short, not even five feet tall, and a bit heavy. Whenever she wanted to have a window, which was built very high, opened or closed, she asked the tallest girl in the class to do it for her and then she said, "The best thing about being short is: you get others to do things for you." How could I forget such wise advice?

By the time I finished the Scottish School I was almost twenty-one.

French Cuisine

After Scottish School and before college, I spent a couple of leisure years at home. I traveled back and forth to Cairo to visit with my grandmother and aunt and uncles. At other times I'd meet with friends, go shopping, and help my parents entertain at home. A lot of time was also spent at the movies or concerts, or any pleasurable activities. I had not a care in the world .

Toward the end of summer of 1955, one of my friends called me to see if I would like to join her in attending a cooking class. The French Franciscan nuns were offering a three-month French cuisine program, and at the very last session we would learn how to bone a whole chicken without tearing the skin. This sounded very interesting. Right away I thought of my best friend, Anahid, who had recently been married. I sent her a note with Abdo, our servant, about it and she also joined us.

Most of us had household help, either a servant or a maid. Some came for the day and went home for the night. Others, who were from out of town, stayed round the clock and were available to help at evening dinnertime. We always had a servant who slept in our home. His duties included keeping the home clean, washing the dishes, and running errands, such as taking the clean laundry to the store to be pressed, doing the daily grocery shopping, etc. Mother would tell the servant what we needed and he would memorize it by counting the number of items. Then Mother would give him some money and off he would go. Upon his return, he would give back the change after having gone through the list and the cost of each item.

He was also a messenger. Most homes did not have telephones. If you needed to call the doctor, you went to a neighborhood store, paid two *piasters*, and made your call on their phone. What if you wanted to talk with a friend or relative who did not live too far? You wrote a note and the "mobile telephone" took it to the friend on foot. You also gave him instructions as to whether he needed to wait for an answer to bring back or not.

Much of what we do in the home now, such as baking, laundry, ironing, etc., was done outside the home then. All baked food was prepared at home and then sent to the bakery where, for a few piasters, they would do the baking for us. In those days, very few people had ovens at home. We had countertop stoves fueled by *butagaz* on which we did the cooking. We sent any dishes that needed an oven—desserts as well as roasts—to the bakery. The baker would place our food in the big commercial ovens with the bread and an hour or two later we would send the servant to get the finished dish.

With Mother doing the cooking and the servant doing the

rest of the household chores (minus the laundry, for which the washer woman came on a weekly basis), I did not have too much to do. This culinary class would offer me the opportunity to learn to use an oven myself.

I wanted to learn fancy French cooking and baking, and this was heaven sent. In anticipation of the cooking classes, I bought several ovenproof dishes—Pyrex pans and platters.

Three times a week my two friends and I went to class. It took us about half an hour on the bus. The classroom had six ovens placed against the walls and there were no more than six students—one oven for each one. The instructor, one of the nuns, had a list of five or six recipes per session. We could choose one or two recipes to prepare that day, pay for the ingredients provided by the school, and then copy any remaining recipes that interested us.

I became an expert at preparing a variety of sauces: *roux, béchamel.* I also learned various French pastry methods such as *pâte brisée, pâte à choux,* and *pâte feuilletée.* After the cooking and baking we could either taste each other's preparations or take ours home.

I often took a dessert home for the evening's guests. My father was delighted. He was always very proud of any accomplishment of mine. He loved to brag about my schoolwork and now he started to brag about my culinary talents. He kept promising his friends, "My daughter will prepare such and such for us tonight. You are all invited to come and taste." But what I brought home was just in addition to what Mother would have prepared during the day. She was an excellent cook and dessert baker. In spite of the French Cuisine course, I never achieved the artistry of her cake decorations. Yet having contributed to the evening's degustation with my very own "new" item gave me so much pleasure. I could now offer *my* recipe for the ladies who wanted a copy of it.

Two specific baking/cooking lessons from that period stand out. First, I learned that when you prepare a flan, you have to be very gentle with it, especially when it is still warm. One time I decided to make one in a flat Pyrex dish because my parents were having friends over that evening. After our class, we three young friends took the bus to return home, carrying our preparations of the day. I held the flan as securely as possible. When I got home, I proudly opened the cover to show my masterpiece to Mother, and what did I find? The whole thing had broken up into small pieces no larger than the size of a quarter. Even though the buses were quite modern and jostling was at a minimum, still the slight shaking created a flan that resembled a jigsaw puzzle.

Then there was the boning of the whole chicken. Until this class I had not done much in the kitchen other than help mother with very minimal tasks such as adding the flour to her pound cake recipe by the spoonful. I had never even touched any kind of raw meat—not fish, not lamb, and certainly not chicken. It felt cold, slimy. It gave me the shivers.

Well, I closed my eyes, promised myself I was going to do it, and touched the raw chicken. It took one whole hour to remove all the bones without tearing any part of the skin. When it was done, I was surprised to see this lump of chicken meat that had no shape and was a whole lot smaller than when we began on it. A lesson in cooking? Actually, a lesson in biology as well. We have no shape without our bones.

We filled the cavity with a combination of veal and beef and vegetables and the chicken meat regained its shape. We then simmered the whole thing in a broth. After it cooled, we set it in a vegetable-flavored jelly and let it set in the refrigerator. Then this chicken could be unmolded, sliced, and offered on a platter at a buffet table.

After the classes, I boned a chicken on my own for us at home. My father was so happy with my accomplishment that one day when he came home from work he informed me, with joy in his eyes, that he had invited a few of his friends and their wives to come for a dinner at which his darling daughter would have boned chicken as part of the menu.

I had to prepare two or three chickens to have enough for everybody. You can imagine how long that took.

I still have the original notebook containing all the recipes from 1955.

I am including two of my favorite recipes, first in French exactly as they are in my notebook, then in English with more detailed directions.

Rôti de Saumon
1 boite de saumon (moyenne)
1 noix de beurre
3 oeufs
3 c. à s. de fromage
3 c. à s. de chapelure

Vider la boite de saumon, le nettoyer. Ajouter la chapelure, les oeufs entiers, le fromage rapé, le beurre. Malaxer le tout. Rouler en forme de rôti et l'entourer avec un linge fin préalablement chapeluré. Bien fermer et mettre ½ heure dans une casserole d'eau bouillante salée. Retirer et decouper en rondelles. Servir accompagné soit d'une sauce mayonnaise, soit d'une sauce hollandaise.

Salmon Log
1 can salmon (medium)
1 nut-size butter
3 eggs
3 tablespoons cheese (use any hard cheese, grated)
3 tablespoons breadcrumbs (plain)

Empty the can of salmon, clean the skin off. Add the breadcrumbs, the eggs, the grated cheese, the butter. Mix all together. Form into a log. Place on a double layer of cheesecloth sprinkled with additional breadcrumbs. Tie the two ends well. Place in pan of boiling, salted water for 30 minutes. After removing, allow to cool, remove the salmon from the cheesecloth, slice into about ½ inch rounds and serve with either mayonnaise or hollandaise sauce.

Note: Excellent for a buffet table.

Pâte de Fruits
Pommes
Sucre   *même poids*

Eplucher les pommes, les peser et mettre le même poids de sucre, bien remuer les deux avant de les mettre à cuire sur feu moyen. Tourner sans cesse jusqu'à ce que la pâte se détache de la casserole. Retirer et metre dans un moule légèrement huilé. Laisser prendre au frais et démouler. Découper en petits carrés et passer dans le sucre cristallisé. Mettre en caissettes.

Fruit Paste
Apples
Sugar   Same weight

Peel and core the apples. Weigh them and add same weight of sugar in a pan. Mix them thoroughly. Cook at medium heat, stirring constantly until the liquid evaporates considerably and the paste detaches from the sides of the pan. Remove from heat and spread in a flat, lightly oiled pan. Allow to cool off completely. Unmold, cut into small squares, and roll into coarse, crystalized sugar. Put each square in a candy paper cup.

Note: Instead of pouring into a pan and cutting into squares, I prefer to make small balls, the size of a small nut, by hand, roll them into the sugar, then allow to cool completely in candy paper cups. Be careful, it is very hot. Allow to cool off enough to be able to handle it safely.

1952-1956

In February of 1952, demonstrations began in Cairo. Mobs set
fire to famous hotels, businesses, even homes. The streets were
full of the demonstrators shouting and swearing with blood in
their eyes. Public transportation came to a halt, schools bused
their students to their homes immediately (though some were
on the road for hours because of the crowded streets and the
general chaos), businesses closed their doors, people locked
their homes and tried not to be out on the streets. This went on
for several days until the government was able to stop it.

As soon as the news arrived in Alexandria, parents took
their children home from schools, stores closed, panic reigned.
Schools remained closed for two months. I was in my senior
year at Deutsche Schule der Borromäerinnen (the German
nuns school I attended from 1947 to 1952), looking forward to
graduation. We found out later that the same fate had awaited
Alexandria also, but the governor had got wind of it early on
and prepared a good plan of defense, so we were spared.

My parents were starting to plan our summer trip to Cyprus.
Mother, Ohannes, and I were to sail first, and during the last

couple of weeks of the vacation Father would join us and we would all return home together. Until that time, Ohannes and I were on Mother's passport as minors. Just a week before the date of departure, the passport office informed us that we were considered adults now and should have our own individual passports. Since there was not enough time for us to get our own passports before the date of departure, it was decided that Mother would go by herself—tickets were purchased already—and we would follow later. Even though Mother was not comfortable with the idea, she agreed because one of her cousins and his family were also planning to travel to Cyprus with us. She had company for the trip and for when they reached Limassol.

One week later, on June 23, 1952, Ohannes and I were on our way. There was an unusually large number of military airplanes in the sky that day and we were wondering about them, but we didn't pay too much attention and went about our own plans. Here we were, the two of us, soon to be seventeen- and nineteen-year-olds, traveling by ourselves and feeling so grown up.

After two days of travel—the ship stopped at Port Said overnight—we reached Limassol and were met by Mother and her cousins in a very anxious state, asking us what the revolution had been like. We had no knowledge of any revolution until we realized what the unusual air traffic had been about.

The revolution of Egypt, which put an end to the kingdom and declared the country a republic, had begun the day we left, banishing King Farouk in a surprisingly quiet way. No blood was shed; no one was harmed. The Army was in charge with the three leaders: Mohammed Naguib, Gamal Abdel Nasser, and Anwar Sadat.

At the end of the summer, we returned home from our vacation and life continued without major changes, except that some street names honoring royal family members were starting to be replaced with names like Liberty or Freedom. But one year later, Mohammad Naguib was placed under house arrest and Gamal Abdel Nasser took charge of the country. I paid little attention to details and what was happening behind closed doors, but I was looking forward to casting my vote in elections that were promised, just like in other republics of the world, specifically the United States.

Several years before, Father had bought a parcel of land in Ibrahimieh, a very nice middle-class section of the city, well known for its large Greek community. In 1954 he built what had been his dream: a four-story building with two apartments on each floor, ground-level stores on the north, east, and south sides of the building, and a very large public garage on the west at least four times the size of all the rest. We occupied one apartment on the second floor and all the rest were rented, including the garage.

At this point, I decided to give up my plans of further education abroad. Father's expenses were very high and I did not want to add more financial burden.

In 1955, Ohannes started his studies at the newly established Haigazian College in Beirut, Lebanon, with the intention of transferring to the American University of Beirut. That summer Mother and I went to Beirut to be with him. It was a wretched time for me. I hated the city, which was humid, hot, and quite old-fashioned—nothing compared to our beautiful Alexandria. One could not buy anything in any store without having to bargain for the price. We always felt that no matter how smart we thought we had been, we were cheated.

We stayed in Beirut for about one month, then went to the mountains. This was better. The air was fresh with the smell of the pine trees, and the hotels, built in the forests, were also full of other visitors who provided good companionship and good conversations. After a couple of months, we returned to Beirut and again to the unpleasant and stifling heat and humidity. My mother was busy making sure that my brother's wardrobe was in good condition and we got to meet some of his friends and professors. The following year Ohannes got accepted at the American University and went to live at the boys' hostel across from AUB, called University Christian Center.

Mother and I sailed back for Alexandria and I vowed never to get myself in a situation of having to live in that awful city for a long time.

In October of 1956, I went to Cairo to visit my grandmother and my mother's brothers and sister. I stayed for about one month and had a wonderful time. Uncle Garo was married and my Néné and Hagopig lived with him and Tante Zabel. They had an apartment on one of the major thoroughfares of the city, renamed El Horreya Avenue. *Horreya* means "freedom" in Arabic. It used to be called Malika Nazli—Queen Nazli— so named after King Farouk's mother, but after the 1952 revolution, as things started changing so also did street names that had honored members of the royal family and other *pashas* and *beys*. The apartment had a large verandah and we often sat there to drink Turkish coffee and eat cookies.

At other times we went to one of the beautiful Cairo public gardens. Tante Zabel used to get season tickets to the visiting Italian Opera and the Bolshoi Ballet from Russia. While I was there, I attended a performance of *Carmen*, as well as *Swan Lake* by world-famous prima ballerina Maya Plisetskaya of the Russian Bolshoi Ballet. I became one of her most loyal admirers.

Vartoug (short for Vartouhi, which means "rose") and her family lived in the heart of the city in a very large, six-story-high apartment building. There were a variety of shops at the street level and the building had an elevator as slow as everything else in the Middle East. It was in the old style with glass walls and open shaft; you could see all around you. The more modern buildings had modern elevators with the shafts enclosed in concrete and only the door had glass windows.

The shops at the street level included a travel agency where I would spend hours browsing the brochures for different countries and daydreaming. I had picked up a couple of leaflets about New York City, one of which had pictures of the Little Church Around the Corner.

(Years later, when I arrived in the United States, I spent some weekends in New York City with my college friend Aida and her family who had come from Aleppo, Syria. Aida was dating Jack, whom she later married. Jack was born and grew up in Queens and he often gave us sightseeing rides. One time, after he had whisked us through Rockefeller Plaza, Chinatown, and Greenwich Village, he asked me if there was something else I wanted to see. I said, "I want to see the Little Church Around the Corner." He had never heard of it. He asked around, found out where it was, and took us there. I still remember how delighted I was to visit it and enjoy the black woodcarvings resembling roses. We learned from the attendant on the premises that movie stars went there to get married when they did not want too much publicity. At least that's what we were told.)

As I was having a wonderful time in Cairo one year after my unpleasant Beirut visit, President Nasser was preparing a big surprise for me.

The Egyptian government decided that the Suez Canal

belonged to Egypt and not to England and, breaking the contract that existed, took over administration of it. There followed what was to become the Suez Crisis. We watched the planes flying above our heads, again. I left Cairo and returned to Alexandria immediately.

The country took on an eerie feeling and everyone was subdued. The government started to expel all non-Egyptian nationals. Every day we heard of friends and neighbors who had been ordered to leave the country within twenty-four or forty-eight hours, allowed to take only one or two suitcases with them. Homes were closed up and abandoned. Those who owned businesses closed them up or found some friend or other to take over until further notice. Shock, fear, and panic were beginning to grip us. As Egyptian subjects the Armenians were safe, but we were Christians and who knew what the future might hold?

One day, some time in November when Father came home from work, he told me that I had to leave the country and the only logical way was to go abroad for higher education. He had heard some rumors or news that convinced him that it would be safer if I left the country.

Father went to Beirut to spend the Christmas holidays with Ohannes, and Mother and I went to Cairo to be with her family. When he returned on January 2, 1957, he told me, "I spoke with the president of Haigazian College, Dr. John Markarian, and he agreed to accept you during the second semester of the school year. Get ready, you are going to Beirut in three weeks."

This is how, about one month later, in February 1957, I was on my way to Beirut to spend the following three and a half years in the city I had vowed never to live in.

But it was just as well. As Egypt's politics became more socialistic, Alexandria was neglected and lost its charm and beauty, while at the same time, an International Airport newly built in Beirut helped the city on its way to the sophistication with which it is identified today.

Starting College

In early February 1957, Mother and I flew to Beirut on Air France. It was first time on an airplane for both of us. The weeks before that, Mother and I went into a frenzy of preparations. Fabrics were bought for winter as well as summer; dressmakers were hired; shoes were ordered; and suitcases were filled.

I could hardly believe it. I was going to college and then the university, and I was going to be on my own. Beirut had once been the last place on Earth I wanted to spend a few years of my life, but the part of the city I was to stay in was quite different than what I had seen before. It was imbued with the flavor of the American University of Beirut. Even though I was going to Haigazian College, all the English-speaking colleges, including the then Beirut College for Women, got together for lectures and social activities (including the famous annual International Folkdance Festival) and we all felt part of the same atmosphere. We met the president of Haigazian College, Dr. John Markarian, and his lovely wife, Ruth, as well as their six-year-old daughter, Joanne. We got along very well and made friends right away. At that time, Haigazian had a dormitory only for male out-of-town students. Since I was the only female student from abroad, I had to find accommodations off campus. Dr. Markarian suggested the YWCA, a beautiful brick building very close to the American Embassy, overlooking the Mediterranean Sea. We made arrangements for me to live there. There was a beautiful view from the balcony and my roommates and I, and sometimes other students as well, often went to the Embassy for dinner. The rooms had three beds each and we had use of the kitchen for personal meals. The central hall and the living room were also available for our use and our visitors.

My two roommates were both older than me. One was Lebanese, her hometown one of the mountain villages. She lived in Beirut so she could go to work. The other, Hilda, a bit older than the other one, was from Damascus, Syria. I made friends with both right away.

Hilda had a boyfriend who started a summer school in the mountains in a town called Bahamdoun, famous for the most delicious peaches. That year my brother and I did not go to Alexandria for the summer. Hilda asked me if I wanted to teach English in her boyfriend's school. I was to be paid 250 Lebanese *liras* for the month and a half of teaching. The school was actually a house with four bedrooms. Two were made into classrooms and Hilda and I used the other two as our bedrooms, rent-free. On weekends, Hilda's boyfriend would drive us back to Beirut and return us to Bahamdoun Monday mornings.

I had my first honest-to-goodness paying job!

By now, Egypt had formed the United Arab Republic with Syria, and Egyptians could travel to Syria as easily as they did from one city to the other within Egypt, without passports. My parents decided to go to Damascus for a few weeks and my brother and I were to join them there. When Hilda found out about our plans, she offered for us three to go to Damascus together. She helped us a great deal and when we got there she met our parents and showed us around the city.

Damascus was a bit similar to some parts of Cairo but was more crowded, with the same noisy hustle and bustle of the souks where the small stalls were full of wares.

While in Syria we also went to Aleppo to visit friends. I will always remember the clean, white, two-, three-, and four-story buildings built out of the typical white stones of the region. The streets were clean, the air was fresh, and even the inhabitants were pleasant.

When Ohannes started his college years in 1955, the Egyptian Government allowed my Father to send him sixty Egyptian pounds each month for his college and living expenses. This was the maximum allowed. One pound was worth about eight Lebanese liras, give or take a few piasters, and on a good day up to nine liras. The exchange rate varied daily.

By the time we finished our college years, the Egyptian pound was worth four Lebanese liras.

How did these numbers compare with the American dollar in those days? Each American dollar was worth between three and four Lebanese liras.

Even though before the Egyptian revolution one Egyptian pound was worth five American dollars, by the time 1960 arrived, one pound was equal to one American dollar.

When I started my college, Father was allowed to send me sixty pounds also. But after about two or three months, the government told father that I was a girl and did not need that much money—an allowance of forty pounds was enough for me. It was enough, it is true, but being a girl, I was not expected to have the same quality of life as my male sibling.

Surviving Beirut

One day, many years later in Rochester, New York, a friend gave me a copy of a magazine published by the Armenian Missionary Association of America (AMAA). "For you," is all he said. I opened it and saw that the whole issue was dedicated to Haigazian University of Beirut, Lebanon. There was also an article about how the university began as a two-year college in 1955 and became the university that it is today. The article had one picture, taken in 1958, of the first class that graduated with associate's degrees in June of 1958. The casual look on my face turned to a smile and then a big smile, and with eyes wide open and my face beaming, I said, "Why, I have the original of this picture!" It was a scene of the graduation party at the college.

When I got to Beirut, Lebanon, in February 1957 to start college, I had no idea I was going into another country that was to become a war zone very soon. For three semesters, February 1957 through June 1958, I studied at Haigazian College—the aforementioned Haigazian University. I loved my newfound independence as a young woman and enjoyed having to make my own decisions about my studies and my social life.

But trouble had been brewing in the country and there was always fighting among different factions.

During my sophomore year, the college had rented a flat on the fifth floor of an apartment building (with no elevator) across the street as housing for the seven women students who had come from neighboring countries—Syria, Jordan, Iraq, Iran, Egypt. As we were studying for our finals that last semester of '58, they were fighting with guns on the street below. Fortunately, we did not have to go far to arrive at school—just cross the street. We weren't sure if we would have graduation ceremonies if the situation got much worse. As is evident from the picture in the magazine given to me by my friend, we did have graduation ceremonies during a lull in the fighting.

Public transportation was minimal in Beirut and taxis functioned as mini buses, taking on passengers they found on their routes. One afternoon I was trying to get one of those taxis from downtown to get back to the dorm, but there were few working and all the ones that went by were full of passengers. I started walking toward the college as I had done many times before. I could hear explosions in the distance and they were getting louder and louder the closer I got to my destination. Then I ran into a classmate of my brother's who told me that if I was trying to get to Haigazian, the usual route past the Lebanese President's palace was not the way to go. There was fierce fighting going on there and I should take another route.

*1958. First Graduating Class at Haigazian College.
Dr. Markarian is on the right, second row, with his wife next to him.
The little girl in front is Joanne, their daughter.*

So I changed my path, and having taken a lot longer than usual, I was very late getting home. My resident mates were anxiously waiting for me; they had received news of the fighting and knew that I might be right in the middle of it. Had I not run into that friend, would I have been right in the middle of the gunfight?

My brother and I were going home for the summer vacation soon after my graduation. One morning we were on our way to the bank in one of the taxis. As the cab was turning around the corner of a street, I saw a pretty bathing suit in the window of a department store. I told Ohannes that after the bank we should come back to the store so I could buy it. While we were waiting in the bank for our business, we were delayed by about twenty minutes because of some electrical failure. We suddenly heard a big explosion and everyone got in a panic. Still, we finished our business and left. As soon as we were on the street we found out that the great commotion was at the department store we were heading towards, which fire trucks and police cars were busily hurrying to also. The rebels had parked an open truck carrying cases of glass Coke bottles filled with gasoline at the entrance of the department store, and then they set fire to the truck. The bottles exploded and started a fire. People were coming out of the store covered in blood; others were being carried out on stretchers.

We left for our dorms, thankful for that electrical malfunction at the bank.

We sailed for home soon after and spent the summer in Alexandria.

Come September, we sailed back for Beirut for my brother to continue at the American University and for me to start at Beirut College for Women. Today, this college has grown and is now called Lebanese American University, with several campuses in various towns in Lebanon. All was quiet as the ship docked and we waited for the doctor to come and sign the quarantine papers so the passengers could disembark. And we waited and waited. The civil war had become so dangerous that the government had declared twenty-four-hour curfew. No one was allowed on the streets, not even the doctor to let us off the ship.

We eventually did get off and it was most eerie to go through the empty streets, where usually the crowd was so heavy that people bumped into each other on the sidewalk, and to see all the shops with closed front doors. For a few days I stayed at the hostel where my brother lived, and with a few other students we managed to find some restaurants in the neighborhood that opened for the students and the university staff.

Eventually, the aircraft carrier USS *Forrestal* arrived and some peace was restored, and we started our normal life.

Life is interesting. After the incident of my being late because of the fighting at the president's residence, one afternoon we heard sounds just like anti-aircraft explosions. All the girls were home. I, in my wisdom and vast experience, insisted that everyone should get her handbag, passport, and make sure she had enough money because we might have to run for shelter. Having spent a childhood during World War II, I was no stranger to the sounds of bombs, enemy airplanes, anti-aircraft rat-a-tat-tats, and then the sight of destroyed buildings.

But the girls were not taking me very seriously. And it turned out that they were right. When we looked out the window toward the sea, we found out that the explosions were fireworks. I guess I never lived this one down.

One Memorable Day

I still remember my father's voice, "I don't care whether you are a girl or a boy. If you have a brain in your head and I have the money in my pocket, you and your brother are going to attend the university after your regular schooling and fill your heads with as much knowledge as possible. The day may come when you have to leave this country and all you can take with you is what's in your heads."

My father's family had come to Alexandria, Egypt, from Dikranagerd (Diyarbakir) in Turkey before the Genocide of 1915. Because of my grandfather's declining health, young Krikor, my father, started to work to support his parents at the age of twelve. He learned the tool-and-die business, became a master at it, and started his own business in his early twenties.

Though he left school at such a young age, or maybe because of it, my father never stopped self-educating. One of my fondest memories is of him sitting in his favorite chair in the living room reading on a Sunday night. From time to time he would call us over and read something out loud, something he found interesting or important.

The German high school I attended was close to his workshop, and even though I was registered for the school bus, some mornings he liked to drive me to school himself. During those rides he kept repeating this mantra: that I would further my education in Germany (and my brother in England because of which he was attending the British Boys' School). He filled my head with all the hopes he had for Ohannes and me.

However, life has its way of changing our dreams, or the road to them. It so turned out that Ohannes went to Beirut, Lebanon, in 1955 and started at Haigazian College (Haigazian University today), which had just opened.

Soon after the Suez Crisis of 1956 I started at Haigazian College in February of 1957 and finished the two-year program in three semesters and received an associate's degree in 1958. Then, since Haigazian was only a two-year college, I continued my studies at Beirut College for Women (Lebanese American University today). In 1956, my brother had transferred to the American University of Beirut. In the end, both of us finished our college studies the same year and the same month: June 1960.

Turmoil and new laws continued in Egypt. Ohannes and I had gone to Alexandria for the Christmas holidays of December 1959 and had run into great difficulty returning to Beirut. Those were the days when Egyptians were not allowed to travel abroad just for pleasure. Even though we were students and were trying to return to our schools, we were given unnecessary additional red tape to go through. This had terrified Father that we might not be able to finish our last semester.

To make matters worse, Father's health started to deteriorate. By the time our senior year had arrived at our college and university, he was very sick.

In the spring of 1960, Grace Loucks Elliott, the acting president of Beirut College for Women, stepped down and Frances M. Gray, the new president, was appointed. The inauguration of the new president was to take place on April 8. There were a lot of preparations for this big event. The campus had to be in perfect shape, the landscaping exquisite. The poetry recitations and speeches were rehearsed to perfection. Government dignitaries and presidents and faculty of all the local colleges were invited, as well as family members of the class of '60. Since my parents were in Egypt and planning to come in June for both our graduation ceremonies, I asked Ohannes to attend.

The ceremony was to take place in the auditorium. The faculty, each in his or her own academic dress, was to march down the aisle towards their appointed seats followed by the soon-to-graduate class in their caps (tassels on the right) and gowns. Although we had not officially graduated yet, it was decided that we were close enough to the date to be considered "almost graduates."

1958. At Uncle Garo's home in Cairo.

There was an air of excitement in everything we did during the preparations. We had to continue our courses, finalize and present our theses, and prepare for our final exams; and then we were given this unexpected privilege that had never been done before.

Finally, the day arrived and everything proceeded smoothly just as planned. As we sat in our seats, dressed in our caps and gowns, and listened to the speeches and recitations, my mind started wandering forward. In two months, another ceremony would take place in this same auditorium and I would be in my cap and gown legitimately. And best of all, my parents would be there. I could picture them sitting in the audience, my father exuding pride. I kept telling myself, "Two more months, two more months."

Then the inauguration was over and everyone was leaving for the receptions that followed. Among the dignitaries were Dr. John Markarian and his wife, Ruth. They were looking for Ohannes and me. Dr. Markarian wanted to talk with my brother, so they walked away. Mrs. Markarian asked me to take her to my dormitory room so she could see it.

When we got there, after some small talk, she told me the real reason why they each wanted to talk to us in private.

Dr. Markarian had received a telegram from my Mother.

Father had died on April 6 and been buried on April 7. He was fifty-seven years old.

Mother's message said that we were to continue our studies and not return home .

He never saw the realization of his dreams for us.

FROG LEGS

In my late twenties, I went back to Lebanon as a graduate student at the American University of Beirut. I was living at Bustani Hall, the residence on campus for women graduate students. I met a young woman there who was also from Alexandria, Egypt, like me, and we became fast friends, especially when we found out that we had been flower girls at the wedding of my parents' upstairs tenants. Her name was Isabelle, and she was about one year older than me. But unlike me, she was not a student. She was a refugee and somehow had managed to get herself accepted to reside in the building. She had no identity papers.

Lebanon in those days seemed peaceful on the surface but everyone carried government-issued ID cards stating one's citizenship, occupation, and reason for being in Lebanon. Today, our news is full of the turmoil in the various countries of the Middle East and we are saddened by the number of casualties we hear about. The trouble had started already in the late 1950s when in 1958 the United States Sixth Fleet came to the rescue and calmed things down for a while. I was there.

Many non-Arab Egyptians went there hoping to get Lebanese citizenship or a passage to the United States or any other country that would take them in through various programs that had been created by the United Nations as well as those other countries. These were not the typical refugees of the early 1900s—they were all people of means, educated, capable of starting their own businesses, and most of them had had their personal fortunes smuggled out of Egypt (at a high cost, of course). It was the early 1960s and Egyptian politics were veering toward Russian-style socialism. The comfortable, westernized lifestyle of the Egyptian middle class had been turned upside down after the Suez Crisis of 1956.

One Sunday afternoon Isabelle and I decided to go for frog legs. There was a famous restaurant in the Beqaa Valley serving them. It was about a two-hour drive by bus. I was bored, had no homework, and wanted something different to do. As for Isabelle, since she wasn't even a student, she was ready for an outing at any time.

About two in the afternoon we went downtown and got on the bus. As I remember, it was a very beautiful spring afternoon, and the weather got cooler, cleaner, and crisper as the bus wandered through the winding roads on the mountains. From time to time the bus would stop to either drop off some passengers or pick up new ones as we went through the beautiful villages with the typical stone houses and the famous cedar trees. The restaurant we were planning to go to had become famous for its frog legs. The tables were arranged around a small brook, gurgling along and adding to the unique atmosphere. I'd never had them before and was very excited, because this was the ultimate, newest, in-thing to do—to go to the town of Zahlé and eat frog legs.

Dinner was everything I had expected. The frog legs were delicious and crispy, and we had a wonderfully relaxing afternoon and early evening. Still, we decided not to dilly-dally and started our return trip before sundown. In 1963 Lebanon was no place for two young women to be out late by themselves in these locations far away from Beirut.

Shortly after we started, the bus was stopped by a couple of men on the road. At first I thought they were passengers. But when they came on board we saw their rifles hanging from their shoulders. They started asking the passengers to produce their ID cards for inspection.

"I guess I'll spend the night in prison," Isabelle said.

"Don't worry. I won't produce my papers either so that if you are taken to prison, they'll have to take me as well. You won't be alone."

We had a couple of magazines we were reading. It suddenly occurred to me that we were women after all and chances were that these people would treat us as not very important. They were not going to consider us dangerous. Gambling on this culture, I quietly told Isabelle, "We'll continue looking at these magazines together as though there is something very important we are discussing. We'll pay no attention to them and pretend that we will not be expected to produce any papers."

The two men moved slowly, inspecting IDs carefully. Gradually they reached our row of seats and without even a glance at the two of us passed to the row behind. We continued being our "unimportant feminine sex" until they left the bus, and we started to breathe. The bus continued to Beirut without any further stops.

We never ate frog legs again in the Beqaa Valley.

Part Two

The
Homeland
I Adopted
(And which
adopted me
back)

Why, and How, I Came to the U.S.

In the late 1950s and especially the early 1960s, there was a panic, a frenzy, among the Christian non-Arab population—consisting mostly of the Armenians and the Greeks, as well as some Coptic Egyptians—to leave Egypt and rebuild a life in another country. At the time, the political situation was very tense, almost dangerous, as Gamal Abdel Nasser was immersing the country in socialism. He had taken a great deal of assistance from the Soviet Union in building the Aswan Dam and thus allowed the Soviet philosophy to permeate his regime along with his own corrupt tendencies.

When King Farouk was expelled by the main revolutionary, Mohammed Naguib, during the white revolution in 1952, our lives changed in a way that no one had imagined. We had lived a good, peaceful, abundant life—we, that is, the minority of the population consisting of the Egyptian nobility, old Syrian families, and almost all the non-Arab population who were mostly Christian. There was also a large Jewish community, who had been in the country for many years. The Armenians, most of whom were the survivors or the descendants of the

Genocide of 1915, were under Egypt rule. But the Greeks, the French, the Italians, the English, and the Germans, had their own laws. If a foreign subject got into trouble with the law, he or she was tried according to the laws of his or her own country. This had changed by the time of the revolution, yet this foreign element in Egypt was still the privileged one.

Deep down we knew that this was not fair, but still we enjoyed the comfort and abundance that our host country provided for us. When the revolution first came, in spite of what the future might hold for us, we welcomed the promises of new schools being built for the Egyptian population, education and opportunities for a better life. In our household we encouraged Abdo, our live-in servant, to go to night school and become literate. We followed his progress and encouraged him to go as far as he could.

Then came the Suez Crisis in 1956. This is when our lives changed completely. Almost all of the foreign subjects were expelled from the country. The Greeks went to Greece, the Italians to Italy, the English to England, and so forth. But we, the Armenians, had no Armenia to go to—Armenia was part of the Soviet Union at that time. Even though the majority of us were Egyptian subjects, there were indications that our names and our religion were leading us into a precarious situation.

Shortly after the Crisis, I went to Beirut to attend the university and spent three and a half years there, graduating with a bachelor's degree in Education and English. After graduation in June of 1960, I returned to Egypt and taught English at the American College for Girls in Cairo. But I knew it was temporary; my aim was to leave the country and never return.

It was during my year of teaching in Cairo that the exodus started. Canada opened its doors with unlimited quota for the Egyptian Armenians, and almost every week we heard of another relative or family friend leaving, emigrating.

After my one year of teaching, I returned to Alexandria and stayed with Eby. In 1961 I applied to the Canadian Embassy in Cairo for an immigrant visa for both of us. Her family did not intend to leave for their own reasons and this caused a deep sadness in my mother—impending separation from her family. At the same time, while in Beirut, Ohannes had applied to the United Nations and, under a special program for residents of countries with socialistic governments, was granted entry into the United States, Rochester, New York, to be exact. In Egypt, pleasure traveling was allowed only to women over the age of fifty-five and men over the age of sixty, once a year. Luckily, in 1962 Mother turned fifty-five years old, so she was given an exit visa to visit Lebanon to see Ohannes off.

After my mother's return from Beirut, I received my visa to emigrate to Canada.

Mother had to stay behind until I was settled and working.

80

This of course created a major conflict. She now had one child in the United States and one child on the way to Canada. And she could not leave Egypt more than once a year. Would she ever be reunited with her children? And if so, when?

She stopped smiling. Her sad face followed my every move. Yet she never uttered a word. As I was planning my own emigration, I felt torn between wanting to do the right thing and at the same time not causing her anymore hurt. Whenever I asked for her opinion, she said, "Do what you feel you have to do. I don't want to influence you." But her sadness was telling me exactly what to do. I informed the Canadian Embassy that I had changed my mind and withdrew my application.

I decided to return to Beirut to continue my studies. It was the simplest and surest way of getting out of the country. Since Mother's once-a-year traveling visa had been used up, she could come to join me the following January and then we would apply to the United Nations together and come to join my brother in Rochester. It took me one whole year of red tape to get permission to get my student visa but finally, in October of 1962, I flew to Beirut with four suitcases and twenty Egyptian pounds in my pocket. Mother was supposed to send me the monthly allowance for my studies, just as Father had done before.

The Egyptian authorities kept delaying the permission for my funds to be sent to me. I had no other resources in Beirut, so I applied at Tarouhi Hagopian School for Girls, where I had done my student teaching in 1960. I was accepted and started teaching English part time. This of course infringed on the time available for my studies and I had to take one course less than I had planned. I also did not live on campus, to save money. Instead, I rented a room in one of the apartments in the vicinity of the university. The owner of the apartment was an Armenian widow.

At the end of the second month she informed me that I had to vacate the room the following day because she had rented it to a student from another Arab country. She said, "You, Egyptian students, don't have money like before and I want to make sure that I will not have problems with you." I had not been late in paying the rent but she was not going to take any chances, I suppose. Now I was on the street with four suitcases and nowhere to go.

My best friend Alice, from my college years, lived in Beirut and came to my rescue. She found an elderly Armenian couple almost across from the university. The wife offered to take me in without even consulting her husband, who was at work at the time. It turned out that these were some of the kindest people I have ever met in my life. They wanted to be like second parents to me. But, their home was so small, the only place they could give me was the extension of the living room, which was like a sunroom. Very small and also very noisy, overlooking

82

the street with constantly honking cars. I had no space to be private, do my homework, or correct students' homework. I had to find a new place to live. But I shall never forget them and their kindness.

Eventually, Alice found another lady with a room to rent. This also turned out to be the wrong thing. Finally, I decided that I was going to live on campus. The graduate women's dormitory was new, clean, and peaceful. I told myself that if, in the end, I could not pay for everything with my current teaching salary, the university had to ask for the money from the Egyptian Embassy because I was still an Egyptian student.

Shortly after I made the decision, Mother wrote that she had received permission and was sending the whole year's expenses all at once. What a relief.

Come January 1963, President Nasser changed the law for travelers. Women over the age of sixty and men over the age of sixty-five could now have an exit visa for pleasure once a year. Mother would be trapped for another five years.

Nevertheless, she sent word to me that I should not wait for her. I should go ahead with my plans.

Thus, in October of 1963, I finally arrived in the US.

Thoughts From an Immigrant

When I first arrived in the United States, I lived with my father's cousin, Onnig (John) and his wife, Annig, in New Jersey. Everyone I met wanted to ask me one of two questions:

1. What do you think of Gamal Abdel Nasser and his politics?
2. What do you think of America?

Having just come from an atmosphere of secrecy and keeping your mouth shut for the sake of your and your family's safety, after making sure that all the windows in the room were closed, I had answers for both questions that were partly true and mostly safe.

1. Oh, he's very good for the general population with his free schools and farming opportunities for the villagers.
2. I find that people have the same characteristics and nature wherever they live. People are people.

I did not dare explain that I had come here for the freedom this country promised. I had come here because I did not want to have my mail opened and read by the censors; I did not want a third party listening in on the telephone to monitor the subject of my conversation with a friend; I did not want to end up in jail for having in any way expressed disagreement or even disappointment in the new laws being enacted almost daily.

As for question number two, I did not explain that I had found surprises I did not expect. One thing that left me completely baffled, and it still does, was to see youngsters of perhaps twelve or so years old by themselves on the streets at night. Where were their parents? Why weren't they at home at this late hour?

And then there were the comedians on TV shows who made jokes about the government and elected officials. This seemed so disrespectful to me. But one day, when I became a US citizen, if I disagreed with the government I could say so without the fear of imprisonment. The thought filled me with awe.

It was several weeks, or maybe months, before I realized that the streets were different here. First, there were no cars constantly honking their horns. The avenues were wider, traffic followed rules, and pedestrians were respected. I had never before been in any city—Cairo, Beirut, Damascus, and even some parts of Alexandria—where drivers did not express their impatience and anger without making good use of the horns at their disposal. The roads were quiet here.

Beirut was the worst. There were traffic lights in the city

but no one paid attention to them, so they had stopped using them. They just hung in the middle of the streets, useless, and pedestrians had to take their lives in their hands just crossing the streets. It was amazing how agile these Beirutees were, running in and out between cars, never a scratch on them. There was a lot of shouting by the pedestrians and the drivers, yet everyone got to their destination no matter what. During my student days there, when we went home for our summer vacation, I'd get into the good habit of following the traffic light when crossing the street. Then came September and we were back in Beirut, and I had to relearn how to cross the street like the Lebanese.

In the streets of Beirut, people shouted at each other in anger and it was not unusual to see two people in fistfights for whatever reason.

And then one day I felt peace for the first time in my life. No war. No bombs falling overhead. No need to worry about getting to the shelter. Yes, there was war in which the United States was involved, but it was far away in Vietnam. People talked, people argued, people protested, but it was far away. Even though young Americans were fighting and dying in a foreign land, the inhabitants of the United States were living in peace. It was such a difficult concept for me. I had lived through World War II, the 1948 War with Israel, the 1952 Egyptian Revolution and establishment of a republic, the 1956 Suez Crisis, and, in 1958, the chaos of the start of the civil war in Beirut: constant fighting and gunfire in the streets while we studied for our classes on the fourth floor of our dorm.

It was 1963, and I was finally living in peace.

My First Job in the U.S.

I wrote to Ohio State University requesting application forms. I had seen a flyer on the bulletin board in the office of the Dean of Women Students at the American University of Beirut, offering a fellowship to continue my studies started in Beirut: a master's degree in Educational Psychology. I wrote from New Jersey asking for the necessary paperwork and naturally gave a New Jersey return address. Shortly thereafter, Eby sent me a whole package of application papers. They had been mailed to my Alexandria address by Ohio State University. As far as the Egyptian government knew, I was supposed to be in Beirut studying, not the US.

I panicked. Mother's safety was being jeopardized. I was in fear of being discovered and imagined that spies were investigating my whereabouts. Ridiculous, yes, but fear has no reason, no logic, when you are running from danger. I had visions of spies at Ohio State sending the information of my "defection" to the Egyptian government, which put my mother in a dangerous position. Instead of filling the application forms, I wrote another letter to the university and informed them that my plans had changed and I was not going to apply.

Instead, I started to inquire locally about finding a teaching job with only half my master's completed. With the help of friends, I went to Camden, New Jersey, to inquire about my eligibility and certification to teach at the high school level. That did not work out. I needed to take more courses and at that time I did not have the money. My funds were still in Egypt.

The next step was to look for a job I could qualify for. Any job.

Every Sunday, I would go through the want ads in the newspaper, find two or three possibilities, and jot them down on my notepad. During the next week, I would take the bus from Nutley, get off at Port Authority in New York City, and walk all the way to each address and apply. I did not dare take any local public transportation; I was not familiar with the routes, and I did not know where I might end up. So, I walked and walked. At each agency, there was a good excuse for not considering me no matter what the position: I was not a citizen and the job required confidential information; I did not have the experience; and the one that puzzled me the most—I was overqualified. I thought being overqualified would get me the job because I could do it properly. But no, it doesn't work like that.

Eventually, one of my uncles suggested that I apply at Western Electric in Kearney, New Jersey. He said it was a good place to work. They had about 17,000 employees doing manufacturing and office work. He drove me there one morning and I filled an application form. I checked off the box for "clerical" instead of "shop."

There were perhaps more than fifty applicants in a very large hall, waiting to be interviewed.

The first thing I was asked to do was take some aptitude tests, which were to determine my comprehension of the English language. Then came more tests, checking my manual dexterity. By now it was about noon. A gentleman came to me and said, "You qualify to work here, but with your background, do you really want to work in the shop?"

"I did not apply for shop, I applied for clerical," I replied.

He looked at my application form, which was in his hands, and said, "You're right. But now we have to give you some more tests." Having studied about IQ tests during my college and university years, I recognized immediately what they were.

I was led into the office of a lady, who was most probably the human resources specialist. She told me that there was one position she could offer me, filing clerk in the billing department with an entry-level salary of $66 per week.

"You mean to tell me that in this company where you employ about 17,000 people, you have only a filing clerk's position open?"

"Yes," she said.

"I'll take it."

Then she got on the phone and called the supervisor of the billing department, telling him, "I have a woman of superior intelligence for your opening."

I have always marveled at that strange moment: being openly described as having superior intelligence while being offered such a basic position.

But at least I had a job.

I used to take a bus from Nutley to Newark then change to another bus to take me to Kearney. There were only two buses in the morning and then in the evening on this route especially for Western Electric employees. If you missed both, you had to take a cab or miss a day's work, which would not be good on your employee record. I'll never forget the morning when the snow delayed the bus to Newark. By the time I got there the Kearney buses had already left. I took a cab and, even then was late. I was forgiven only because I was new to snow and this would serve as a good lesson to start out earlier in the wintertime.

As time went on, I made friends with a young woman who had a car and had formed a carpool. She offered me to join her.

Life is very interesting, I keep telling myself. The paths that we are led onto often bring such unexpected encounters. The first day at my job my boss took me around the department and introduced me to the members, about ten to twelve of them.

One of the ladies, as soon as she heard my name, said, "Oh, I know you. You are my cousin, living with John and his family."

My paternal grandmother (Hamama) had three sisters and three brothers who had all emigrated to the US. Uncle John, with whom I was staying, was the older sister's son, best friends with my father. This one, Alice, was the daughter of the youngest sister, who had actually been the youngest of all the siblings and had arrived here with her mother at the age of thirteen. I had heard about all these persons and seen some pictures that meant not much to me while I was young. Now they were becoming real and filling out those pictures.

As time went on, we became great friends, I visited them many times, and I got to know my great-aunt, her husband, and Alice's younger sister, Lucy. Eventually both sisters came to visit us in Rochester several times.

In the spring of 1964, Uncle John and his wife decided to sell their house and move to a smaller place. I did not want to be a burden to them but I was not earning enough to be on my own in Nutley. In July, Western Electric closed for two weeks for vacation. I took this as my opportunity to go to Rochester, New York—where my brother lived—and see if I could find a job there.

Ohannes had become engaged to Mary Ann and they were planning to get married in May 1965. I arrived in Rochester by Greyhound bus and as my brother met me at the station, the first thing he said was, "Mary Ann and I will be settling in Rochester and we think it will be a good idea for you to come to Rochester also. At first we can rent a small apartment for you and me, and when I move out after the wedding, you'll be able to be on your own."

I started to apply to jobs in Rochester right away, such as Kodak and the Public Library. Kodak asked for "office skills," which I did not excel in; and the Public Library, even though they at first offered me a job, withdrew the offer when I expressed that I was planning to continue my studies and complete my half-finished degree.

Interestingly, my stay in Rochester lasted more than two weeks because the famous Rochester Riots of that year prevented me from going to the Greyhound bus terminal to return to New Jersey.

I was late getting back to work. It didn't matter, because even though I hadn't yet secured a new job, I gave my resignation as of September first.

Ohannes drove to New Jersey the weekend following Labor Day, we piled my several suitcases and a trunk full of household items I had had shipped from Beirut into his car, and we came to Rochester. He had rented a one-bedroom furnished apartment on University Avenue, number 477. It was one of those very large homes converted into small convenience apartments. The inside looked like a maze of hallways. I always wondered what

93

would happen if there were a fire. And sure enough, after we had both moved out, there was a fire at number 477 and the building burned down completely. The space is now a parking lot.

The bedroom had one dresser and a double bed. The living room had a sofa, a couple of armchairs, a small table, and one wall that was all glass. The kitchen was so small that I could stand at the sink, turn around, and be at the stove and refrigerator. But that first winter in Rochester, I enjoyed sitting in the living room and watching the large tree outside the window covered entirely in ice, sparkling as the sun shone.

I slept in the bedroom and Ohannes took the sofa in the living room.

I took one week to organize our belongings and the following Monday I walked to Midtown Plaza to look for a job.

The Proofroom, and On

One week after arriving in Rochester, I walked to Midtown Plaza to inquire about applying for a teaching position. At that time the New York State Employment Agency was located on the fifth floor of Midtown Plaza's offices building. I was told that by then, September, teaching jobs were all filled. But they had just received a request for a copyholder at a law book publishing company in town. It was something to do with proofreading, the interviewer said. He didn't know what it was exactly. He suggested that I look into it for now, and return to the Employment Agency in the spring when teaching positions for the following year would be available.

Does not hurt to try, I thought.

He also gave me the name of the supervisor, Mrs. Clara Yost. The Lawyers Co-operative Publishing Company being not too far from Midtown—actually just on the other side of the Genesee River—I walked over the bridge, found the building, and asked to see Mrs. Yost.

The interview was positive. Mrs. Yost told me that it was an entry-level position that paid $66 a week. I had started at the same pay in Kearney, New Jersey, and reached $75 per week by the time I left—I'd been there only seven months. At Western Electric I had joined the union, as I was told I had to, and this had prevented my supervisor from advancing me according to my ability. He explained that if I had not joined the union, he would have placed me in a different category, which would make me eligible for promotions on merit instead of seniority.

I asked Mrs. Yost if they had a union.

"No, we don't," she answered.

"I accept the position."

My first day at LCP was October 5, 1964.

And what was going to be a few months' work until I could get back to my beloved teaching became a thirty-year career.

The proofreaders worked in pairs—a proofreader and a copyholder. I started out as a copyholder. When the manuscript and the typeset galleys and pages arrived from the linotype department, the copyholder read out loud to the proofreader from the manuscript we called the "copy." Everything that was on the page, including punctuation and capitalization, were noted. All personal names were spelled out. In other words, the copyholder was the second pair of eyes for the proofreader. The latter followed everything on the galleys or pages and made necessary corrections. This type of proofreading was, back then, considered more efficient in the industry. And it really is.

Without a union to make me wait for my turn for a

promotion, I became a copyholder-proofreader within the first three months, and in another year after that, assistant supervisor in the Proofroom. This position included going over the proofreaders' corrections on the galleys, making sure they were correct, and answering any questions that were raised. If I could not answer the question myself, I went to the lawyer-editor's office and consulted with him or her. Sometimes I worked the problem out with the managing editor. Other times I went to the linotype department to make some style decisions with the supervisor of that department. Linotype was on the second floor, Proofroom on the fourth, and the editors on the sixth and seventh. I was on any floor at any given moment for any sort of problem, talking and making decisions with the proper person. In the end, I got to meet and work with just about everyone involved in the production of our law books.

A few years later I was offered the position of supervisor of the copyreading department. This was where the lawyer-editor's manuscript was read for grammar and correct English. I was trusted with the running of this operation in spite of the fact that I was foreign born, and English (actually, American) was not my primary language. Having worked with most of the lawyers previously helped me in my new position where communication was a lot more frequent.

As the computer age entered the publishing industry, the company's jobs changed also and we transitioned from hot metal to computerized printing. Proofreading was automated, hot metal typesetting became obsolete, and all those employees involved in those departments were retrained to perform in new jobs. Thankfully, no one lost his or her job because of the new technology.

Apart from my day-to-day duties, I got to do some extracurricular assignments during the annual campaigns of the United Way of Rochester. Most years I worked as a solicitor in-house. In 1981, I was assigned by the company to work as a loaned executive for ten weeks with the United Way to help various Rochester businesses organize their own in-house United Way campaigns. And eventually, I was asked to chair our in-house campaign. I loved every minute of it.

All in all, my memories are happy ones. There were always challenging assignments and conflicts of personality, but my priority was always to make sure that I was fair to every employee in my care. I was convinced that if I did the right thing and was fair to every person I dealt with, I could sleep at night with a clear conscience.

Was it difficult to change career goals? Not exactly. I was very happy at LCP and was appreciated for my contribution to the company's operations. I also realized that with my cultural background, I would not necessarily make a good teacher here at the high school level. I just could not connect with the teenagers here. And the sixties and seventies saw so many cultural changes. One of my duties at the company was to guide and train my employees, and that was close enough to teaching.

In 1989 the company was sold and we had to work under new management, which was not easy. We simply did not understand each other. We were constantly criticized and told that we were doing everything wrong. I could not understand how newcomers could tell us what to do without knowing what we did in the first place. My job changed and suddenly I found myself being shuffled from one position to the other. I lost my Proofroom (by then I had become the supervisor of that department). Some personnel were given early retirement packages. I was pretty unhappy and didn't know what to do next. It didn't look as though I was going to be given the opportunity to retire early even though I was by now in my late fifties. I kept praying for a sign to guide me to the right decision.

For the last two or three years our winters were bad and I had driven on icy roads pretty much daily. Every weekend I'd tell Marcel, the man in my life, "I am giving my resignation on Monday." And he would talk me into being a little more patient. One very snowy morning in January 1994, while I was driving to work, suddenly a snow cloud descended on the road. Cars slowed down to five miles an hour with almost zero visibility. I drove through it for about one mile and when I got to LCP, I parked the car, went inside, walked to my manager's office, and told him, "I am giving you six months' notice. I will retire in

July when I turn sixty-one."

And that's how on July 31, 1994, my thirty-year career at The Lawyers Co-operative Publishing Company ended.

1994. My retirement party, with Marcel.

A MOTHER'S DAY GIFT

I had left Egypt for the last time on October 3, 1962. My trip to Lebanon had been allowed because I was going to be studying at the American University of Beirut towards a master's degree in Educational Psychology. However, I had no intention of returning to Egypt. Mother and I decided that, after my departure, in January or February of 1963, she would take her yearly allowable trip to Beirut and together we would apply for our immigration to the United States.

But Gamal Abdel Nasser raised the age limits for travel abroad to: women at age sixty and men at age sixty-five. Now Mother could no longer travel, because she was only fifty-six. She sent word to me that I should not waste time waiting four more years in Beirut until she could join me legally. I should go on with my plans to come to the United States. This was a very hard decision for me because, as we had been learning from the constant changes of the laws, there was no guarantee that in a few years the age limits might not be raised again. At the same time, there was constant trouble in Lebanon. Unrest, pretty much like civil war, was ongoing. At any given moment there could be gunfire in the streets and you had to take cover. Beirut was not the ideal place to wait for several years until Mother's arrival. I decided to take her advice and hope for the best. I arrived in the United States on October 17, 1963, not knowing if I would see my mother ever again.

Four years later, the age limits did not change in Egypt, and in 1968, at age sixty, Mother applied for a visitor's exit visa, was given permission, and let us know that she would be arriving here in the month of May. We were all very happy, to say the least. We were anxious to be reunited after so many years. I had just been promoted at work and was very proud of myself. I wanted Mother to be proud of my achievements. I rented an apartment on my own and moved out of the one I was sharing with a roommate. My brother wanted Mother to meet Mary Ann and to get to know her daughter-in-law. They were expecting their first child, but the news had yet to reach Egypt.

We traveled to New Jersey to stay with our Uncle John (who was actually Father's first cousin) and his wife, Annig, for the weekend. On the date of Mother's arrival, a Saturday, we all drove to Kennedy Airport to meet her. As Mother got off the airplane, Mary Ann hugged her mother-in-law. Her first words were: "Mother, you are going to be a grandmother!" The following day was May 10, Mother's Day.

Mother always said that had been the best Mother's Day present she had received, to be reunited with her children and be told of the arrival of her first grandchild. It had also been the best Mother's Day present for us to have our mother safe, with us, and sharing our lives for the next twenty years.

The Stepchild

One evening, while the parish council of the Armenian Church of Rochester was meeting at my home, the phone rang. When I answered, I heard a voice that sounded very much like Maurice Chevalier. The caller introduced himself as Marcel Clerentin in French and told me that a mutual friend had given him my name. He wanted to meet me and invited me to the movies the following Saturday to get to know each other. I told him that I had a meeting going on at my house at that moment and couldn't talk any further. If he would leave his phone number with me, I would call him later.

I wanted to find out more about him from our mutual friend, who happened to be at my house that very moment. But all I found out was that he was a widower, and very kind. They were both volunteers at the Genesee Hospital and worked together once a week. I thought this Marcel Clerentin sounded legitimate and worth a try.

We did go to the movies the following Saturday, and I was delighted to have an opportunity to practice my French, which had become rusty after not being used for more than twenty years. He did not tell me his age, only that he had been retired for ten years from Genesee Hospital.

After the movie outing, we saw each other a few more times. He certainly was very persistent in his attentions to me. Right away he started talking about marriage. I panicked. I was in my fifties and had never been married. I had been on my own for so long, and no man had ever told me what to do except for my father, who had passed away when I was in my twenties. Marcel seemed to be a bit too strong for me. And persistent, for sure. I wasn't about to embark on a new experience like marriage after having been on my own for so long with a person I did not know very well yet.

I used to find a bouquet of wild daisies at my door when I came home from work, which he had gathered during the day. Did he know that daisies are one of my favorite flowers?

Other times I'd find him at my house, on a ladder, cleaning the gutters.

He insisted that we go on a vacation together—anywhere I wanted!

He didn't know how costly such an offer could be for him, because "anywhere" with me might end up in Australia, or India, or Alaska, or a South African safari, or even the moon, had the choice been available.

His persistence eventually wore me down and we settled on a two-week train ride to Toronto, Montréal, and Québec

City. It was September and the best of weather for such a trip. We visited friends of mine in Toronto and some of my cousins in Montréal. In Québec City, the longest stay, we were on our own. That's where I learned to drink Beaujolais and heard the story of his childhood. I also learned his age. He was seventy-eight.

Marcel was born on January 10, 1911, the youngest of three children, in a small town in the northwestern part of Picardie, in France. When he was six years old, his mother died during the Spanish flu epidemic. The three children were sent to live with different relatives. Marcel went to his maternal grandparents. He had pleasant memories of those years when he used to go into the woods with his grandfather, a woodcutter, and learn about nature and all the big and small creatures around him. He was very knowledgeable about nature, which he loved.

Those happy days came to an end two years later when his father remarried and Marcel came to live with the new family. His sister and brother remained with the other relatives. His father's second wife was a widow with two children of her own, her husband having died during World War I.

Marcel's life changed drastically—suddenly he became the stepchild in his own father's home. The stepmother was the typical fairytale-style harsh woman who treated the spouse's children from the previous marriage with no kindness. His responsibilities ranged from starting the fire in the morning, to feeding the chickens, to washing the dishes, to running errands, to cleaning the kitchen floor. He had to do all these and more, and also was told that he was no good. If he didn't do his duties properly, he often received a beating, while her own children were pampered—even fed with more nutritious food. Upon the children's return from school, his stepmother used to give her own two children slices of bread with butter and jam, but all Marcel got was a piece of bread smeared with some lard. The two others were also given daily doses of cod liver oil to help them grow up strong, but Marcel was not given any.

He didn't even have proper clothes to keep him warm. Marcel went to school dressed in flimsy clothes and wooden shoes, summer or winter.

There is a humorous story he told me, which is terribly sad in reality.

As was customary for the inhabitants of the town, Sundays the family would go to the patisserie (pastry shop) after church to visit with friends and to enjoy eating pastries, dressed in fine clothes and shoes that Marcel had shined for everyone. But Marcel had to stay home by himself, prepare the meal, and do more chores.

Well! He decided to get even with his stepmother. Since he was all alone with no one to spy on him, he'd get the bottle of cod liver oil and gulp down quite a bit to his heart's content. As bad as it tasted, it was nothing compared to the stubborn determination and satisfaction of getting even . Now he felt that he was not left out of getting the nutrition that his stepsiblings received.

As he told me this and other sad childhood memories, I could picture in my mind the little urchin in his shirt and pants with bare feet with no one to love him.

Québec City will always be a special place for me. As I kept hearing all these stories about the poor child who had become a stepchild in his own father's home, who was missing his own mother and trying not to forget her as her image in his memory was fading away, the mother inside me swelled up with anger toward such cruelty. That's when Marcel achieved his goal. All my love poured out to him and I fell in love.

LIFE WITH MARCEL

So I learned to drink Beaujolais, had red wine with every dinner, and enjoyed a life of bliss for the next eighteen years, interspersed with occasional fireworks of personality clashes and a generational gap I had not expected. After all, Marcel was more than twenty-two years older than me and his childhood and young life experiences had been totally different than mine. Just because he looked and acted younger than his age did not mean he would actually be closer to my peers in his outlook on life. Until we met we had lived totally different lives. Yet my exposure to French at an early age and my knowledge of French customs while growing up in Alexandria helped bridge the gap.

In spite of the tremendous love inside my heart waiting to explode and engulf a family, husband, and children, I never married. I became a single career woman, not by choice but by the way life presented itself and led me on to other paths. And in my fifties I found the relationship that became my "marriage," as I define the term, not as defined by law or religion or society's mores.

I always maintained, and still do, that a real marriage does not need a piece of paper stating the status of two people together. A solid and true marriage is the promise of two persons to each other to build a life together, love each other, be true to each other, and form a family. I remember telling this to a friend a long time ago and being told, "What about the sanctity of the relationship, the blessing of God?" Yes, I believe in God's blessing. And I also believe that a union as I have defined it, if truly and faithfully lived, is blessed by God.

Marcel and I formed a marriage of our own, respecting and appreciating each other. I had no children of my own but he had a stepdaughter, step-granddaughters, and great-granddaughters. We loved his family and my brother's family with devotion. Marcel's own siblings and their offspring were in France and unfortunately I never met them. He visited them several times throughout his life and only once or twice after we met.

As time went on, we learned each other's needs, feelings, hopes, and expectations, and settled into a very happy existence. About two years after our first meeting we decided that for the sake of practicality, he should move in with me. I had a four-bedroom Cape Cod-style house and he was spending more time there than at his apartment. He loved to work in the yard—I promise you there was not a single sprout of crabgrass when you looked out of any window—and he was handy with anything that needed attention like a dripping faucet or hanging a picture on the wall where I could not reach, not to mention his skill in the kitchen and his French cuisine. And we now became "a couple." During his Genesee Hospital years, he had become a certified electrician. With this skill, he wired the whole first floor so any music I played on the stereo could be heard in every room.

Before coming to the United States, Marcel had worked at the Pernod factory as the chief accountant. He was amazing with figures. We often did our grocery shopping together. When we were finished, Marcel would line up the items on the cashier's belt with taxable and nontaxable items separated. He would have already figured out the total we owed and given the cashier the cash, not a charge card, then would say, in his French accent, "You owe me so much change." The poor cashier would be so confused, first trying to figure out the accent and then being expected to give back change the cash register hadn't figured out yet.

I was still working at that time and it was wonderful for me to come home to a homemade dinner with some wine. He loved to cook his recipes and he prepared the best *crème brûlée* I have ever tasted (better than mine). While he enjoyed my occasional Armenian recipes, I was more often treated to his cuisine of Provence.

One day I came home to find a beaming face greeting me, waiting for me to discover two platforms he had built for me. One was in front of the kitchen sink and the other in front of the washing machine and dryer in the basement. They were about one foot wide, thirty inches long, and five inches high, covered with remnants of carpeting left behind after some renovation. I still use them every single day, and I bless him every single time I step on them.

We spoke French with each other, which helped keep the language alive for me. In return he loved to ask me the meaning of a new English word he came across in his endless reading. One of his favorite destinations was the public library and he made good use of both English and French books he found there.

Marcel blended in with my Armenian community and loved to go to church with me. I liked that I did not have to explain to him who the Armenians are, what our history is, and what the Armenian Genocide of 1915 was. During his years at the Pernod factory in Marseille he had met many Armenian workers (he remembered the women better than the men) and had learned all of that from them, actual survivors.

One month after I retired from my work, we drove to Florida with the intention of finding a home to buy and move there permanently. We both wanted to be near the sea. A dear former coworker of mine had retired to Melbourne and we had kept in touch. We decided to do the same. Sure enough, we found a beautiful retirement community with manufactured homes (fancy term for fancy mobile homes) with a swimming pool, enough walking lanes, and bingo every Tuesday night. Three weeks later we returned to Rochester, I put my house on the market, and we started our plans. Right after Christmas, Marcel drove to Melbourne by himself in his car packed to the top with household items he would need, and I remained in Rochester until my house would sell. As the months went by, my house was not selling, so I simply traveled between Melbourne and Rochester and remained in each location for a month or two.

I finally decided to keep my house. It was practical for me to have my place to stay in because I never changed my residency from Rochester to Melbourne and continued to travel every few months back and forth.

Melbourne turned out to be a popular city in Florida, where many Rochesterians retired and formed a community with at least one yearly picnic during which they serve "white hots" (a type of hot dog) flown in from Rochester especially for the event. Even though we enjoyed the warmth, the constant blue sky, and the company of my friend from LCP, we realized that we actually missed the snow, as well as our families. Our families did come to visit, but that was not enough. And I hated the lizards crawling on the walls of the garage, the unexpected insects that had come into the home and were hiding inside the shoes, the garden snakes crawling around, and the rain and hurricanes. So, we sold our pretty home in Melbourne and returned to Rochester.

We did a lot of traveling within the United States and abroad. We took some memorable cruises and flew to Europe and even to Armenia. Some stand out in my mind because of various bits of conversations or other incidents.

One time, we flew to Tucson, where a bus took us to the hotel. From then on a mid-sized bus transported the participants of the trip to scenic locations and to other cities. The group of about eight to ten couples blended together very well with lots of evening cocktails and storytelling and recounting of the experiences of the day. We visited Prescott, Sedona, and the Grand Canyon where Marcel took a helicopter ride, and where one morning we watched the sun rise over the Canyon. The trip ended in Phoenix, from where we flew back to Rochester. Marcel bought me some beautiful pieces of Native American jewelry in Sedona that still bring me joy every time I wear them.

In 1993 we drove to Wisconsin to attend the fifty-fifth birthday celebration of Mary's (my best friend from German high school days) youngest brother, who lives in the US. All the siblings were coming from Germany. I had known all the family back in Alexandria, so we were invited to join the celebrations and spend a week with them. This trip was by car. On the open highways going west, Marcel stepped on the gas pedal to his heart's content. At one point, he was going at close to eighty miles per hour.

He turned to me and asked, "Are you afraid of the speed?"

"No, I am glad you're not at ninety miles per hour," I replied.

Next thing I knew, he was driving at ninety. He loved to live dangerously.

I can't even remember where we were going on our first plane trip but I will always remember our conversation that started with Marcel saying that he hoped the plane would crash.

Appalled, I turned to him and asked, "How can you think of such a thing?"

"I have experienced many things in my life, but never a plane crash," was his reply.

We loved to travel with the Automobile Club's organized group trips by land and by sea. They had what were called President's Cruises and this was one of them. We flew to Acapulco, where we stayed overnight, and in the morning gathered in the open yard of the hotel with our luggage, meeting other travelers and waiting for the bus that was to give us a tour of the city and then drive us to the cruise ship. While I sat with another couple, Marcel went for a walk and when he returned he was soaking wet, head to toe, with his hand gushing blood all over. He had fallen in one of the fountains and cut his hand on the marble edge of the pond. We needed emergency care. I shall always be grateful to the fellow passenger who stayed with us, giving me the support I needed to make decisions in getting Marcel help. The Club's escort was also of tremendous assistance. She found a doctor's office close by where Marcel's wound was stitched and necessary instructions given to me. We even managed to take the bus tour of the city that had been planned before boarding the ship. During the whole cruise his left hand was in bandages and he basked in the attention of everyone he met who asked him what had happened.

About seven years into living together, we decided that the house had become too big for us, and I could tell he was having a hard time keeping up with some of the maintenance. We decided that I should sell it and move into a condo and he return to an apartment. We were still "married" and spent every opportunity together, especially the weekends.

Shortly after the change, he gave up driving. He was eighty-nine. I had been wondering how I was going to approach the subject of his giving up the car, when he made the decision on his own. He told me that one day as he was driving he suddenly realized a fire truck behind him—he had not heard the sirens. He knew it was time to stop driving before he got into a major accident. I was so grateful for his wisdom. But now all the driving was on me. Summer weekends he took the bus from Midtown and came to Fairport. In colder weather, I picked him up. Sundays I always drove him back to his apartment. We also spent time together during the week for other fun activities, for movies or dinners, or meeting with friends. I also drove him to all his medical appointments.

The weekends in particular are special times in my memory. If we didn't have a dinner reservation at a restaurant, which became less frequent as time went on, we went grocery shopping. Sometimes he helped me cook dinner, and sometimes he did the cooking. I always prepared his favorite Southern Comfort Manhattans, and he always split open the pistachio nuts for me so I would not break my nails. He would say, *"Tu vois à quoi ça sert un homme?"* ("You see how useful a man can be?") We would then settle for an evening of comfortable conversation on an interesting topic like politics, social customs, or our ideas about life after death.

In 2004, Marcel had to have an operation for colon cancer. The surgeon insisted that he receive chemo treatments just to be sure no cells had escaped the surgery. We met with the oncologist, who was very honest and direct in expressing his hesitation in giving him this treatment. He explained that this was one of the roughest treatments and it would take many months of miserable living. He hesitated treating Marcel because of his age. However, he would if that was what we wanted.

Marcel asked him, "If I don't follow the treatments, how long will it take for the disease to come back?"

"About three years."

"Well, I am ninety-three. That gets me to ninety-six."

As he stood up, he extended his hand to the doctor, shook the doctor's hand, and said, "No, thank you. Goodbye."

Sure enough, about three years later, just before Thanksgiving 2006, the cancer metastasized to his lungs. The doctors gave him about a year to live. But then, one night in April 2007, after we were getting up from dinner at a restaurant, he stumbled and almost fell. Some restaurant guests helped him to my car and I drove around Fairport for about twenty minutes thinking that the fresh air would calm him. I thought he had simply had too much wine. When we got to my condo, he fell again in the hallway. I called an ambulance.

The tests revealed that the cancer had been spreading in his brain as well, and it was full of tumors.

I tried to take care of him at my home but that became harder and harder and he was unable to walk. He was hospitalized. It was the best place for him. He suffered with excruciating pain and it was only there that he could be given relief with strong painkillers.

Fortunately, it did not last long. He was gone in five weeks. He was ninety-six years old.

1989. With Marcel in Rochester.

Once a Week

In the late 1990s, life presented me with a most joyful gift.

Every Friday, my niece Nancy and her husband, Hugh, would stop at my house before going to work. They would leave with me the most precious thing in their life: an eighteen-pound bundle of energy, Katherine, ten months old—together with her portable crib and that day's clothes, and some of her toys and her pram. She arrived wrapped up in her soft, cuddly, warm nightclothes, half-asleep at seven in the morning, and yet with a smile in her sparkling, dark-sky blue eyes.

Once a week I became the guardian of this precious child, who was already quite an individual. I could see her maturing, on a weekly basis, in her comprehension and manual dexterity. I especially loved to see her very definite personality becoming stronger, especially her sense of humor.

The first thing we would do was wave bye-bye to Mommy and Daddy from the window as they left for work in their car. Then I fed her breakfast. Next, I changed her into her day's play clothes. After this, the day's activities varied. One of our favorites was watching the squirrels and chipmunks from the dining room window.

About midmorning we would go for a walk—she in her pram, talking in her own language to the squirrels and the occasional dog passing by on a leash. Gradually, the fresh air would put her to sleep if she hadn't had her morning nap. In the beginning, no matter how tired and sleepy she was, she would not sleep, but deliberately kept her eyes open so she would miss nothing going on in the new environment.

After she woke up, we'd play for a while; we'd sing together, I in my off-key voice, she in her own baby language. She particularly loved the musical stuffed toys she had, and I always had music playing in the house.

She eventually began trying to walk. She would hang on to anything in front of her, stand up, and start to move step by step. Soon she was taking a couple of steps on her own.

I loved to watch her and see how she understood instructions and tried to follow, obey, or disregard what was asked of her. For instance, speeding fast on all fours, she'd notice the plants on the floor to her left and veer toward them. When I told her, "no touch," she'd stop for a second and you could tell that her brain was in high gear, deciding whether to listen to me or not. She'd look at me, then back to the plants, and then attempt moving toward them again. When I repeated "no," she'd turn to her right and follow the path I was not objecting to.

Katherine was such a delight. Seeing her weekly was the

biggest treat of my life. As her head rested on my left shoulder and she patted my back with her hand while I patted her back, explosions of happiness filled my heart and I felt as close to the love and happiness of motherhood as I ever would.

When Katherine was five, I no longer babysat for her regularly. But she still melted my heart when, while I was visiting her home, she would come to me and gently kiss my cheek and in her beautiful, soft voice say, "Auntie, I love you."

When Katherine was fourteen she was still as delightful as the first day I saw her. She played the cello with her brother, Geoffrey, at home and at school recitals. But she has another gift: a gift of writing. She wrote stories and poetry at the drop of a pencil. I am including, with her permission, the following poem she wrote when she was twelve years old.

Thank you, KT (yes, now she is no longer Katherine), for the gift of you.

Every Day A New Day

Every second a new chance
Every minute a new challenge
Every hour a new hope
Every day a new day
Every week a new solution
Every month a new friend
Every year a new resolution
Every lifetime a new story

-KT

In 2016, Katherine graduated from high school and began college.

The Story of the CTS
(That's a Cadillac, You Know)

I learned to drive when I was thirty-three years old, in Rochester. My first car was purchased from Hallman's Chevrolet on East Avenue. Before the Cadillac dreams, way back in Alexandria, I had always wanted to own a Chevrolet. It sounded so beautiful to say "Chevrolet." Say it, reader: see how smooth and elegant it sounds. *Chevrolet*. And yet, the salesman at Hallman's, a friend of my brother's, introduced me to the Buick. He kept telling me that the Skylark was the perfect car for me. This didn't mean anything to me. I wanted a Chevrolet.

I came out of the dealer's as the owner of a 1965 Buick Skylark. In 1967 the Skylark was similar to today's Century, and in those days cars were huge. I became a Buick driver from then on.

Little did I know that Buick had been the dream car of my mother's. When she first came to the United States to live with me, we picked her up in her dream car. During the twenty years that she lived here, I did buy a Chevrolet, but only once. It just was not the car of my dreams anymore, no matter how beautiful it sounded. And during our years together, Eby and I had many wonderful times and trips in my various Buicks.

In my youth I'd been rather impatient with slow drivers, especially the old people who went twenty miles an hour in a forty-mile zone and interfered with the smooth flow of the traffic. I would always complain to Eby, "The bigger the car, the slower the driver," and would add, "especially those Cadillac drivers!" Because, you see, the way I reasoned, the older people were the ones who could afford the Cadillacs.

Eby would say, "I hope and pray that one day when you get old, you will own a Cadillac also." We would both laugh.

I was getting tired of my 1998 Buick Century with 56,000 miles on it, in very good driving condition, and still looking quite new. The practical thing to do was to keep driving this car. The mechanic who serviced my car kept telling me I could drive it till there were over 100,000 miles on it. It was also paid for. If I got a new car, I would have to start with payments and that would be a big chunk out of the monthly budget.

Mid-October I called my brother and told him I was toying with the idea of looking into a new car. Would he come with me to the Buick dealer and see if we could find something for me?

"Why do you want another Buick? Why don't you consider a Honda, a Chevrolet?"

"I feel more comfortable in a Buick; I fit in it better. Though Honda is another one I would consider. Everyone tells me it is a good car."

"What about a Cadillac?"

"No, the time for a Cadillac has passed. It is too expensive and I am too old for one. It is also too big."

"Mine is not a big model, and it is also not expensive; I leased it."

"Years ago I would have loved it, but not any more." When I told Marcel about our conversation, he said, "I would get a Cadillac if I were in your place."

My brother and I made a date and he drove me to the Buick dealer. We saw a few models but I could not make a decision.

We next went to the Honda dealer. As soon as I sat in one of the recommended models, I sank in the seat. The car did not have automatic driver's seat. I had to use a pump to raise it so I could see over the steering wheel. Well, that was out of the question.

Suddenly, the gentle thought in the back of my head forced itself to the front with, "Why not? Why not a Cadillac?"

We drove to the next dealer and the rest is history, as the saying goes.

I was the owner of a CTS.

Dear Mother, now I have the car of my young dreams.

And now it is my turn to drive very slowly, chuckling every time a younger driver, impatient and angry, zooms past this old lady.

Twenty-Eight Years Later

The phone rang. Who would call me on a Sunday afternoon around 1:30?

When I answered the phone, a male voice asked, "Berdjouhi?"

"Yes."

The voice pronounced my name correctly and it sounded vaguely familiar. I tried to place it as my mind started racing through acquaintances and cousins all over the world.

"Do you know who this is?"

"No."

The voice continued in a friendly manner as though we had seen each other only a few days ago. "It's been a long time."

By now, the voice was becoming vaguely familiar, though not as vibrant as I remembered it. Finally I asked, "Bob?"

"Yes."

I froze; in shock. I could not think clearly even though I wanted, desperately, to find just the right thing to say. The one clear thing in my head was: I am so glad I drove Marcel to his home earlier. And where's Bob's wife that he is not afraid to call me in the middle of a Sunday afternoon?

"Don't read anything into this call," continued Bob, "but I think of you often, and I know that many years ago I hurt you. I want to tell you I am sorry."

"Well," I began. *Give me some wise words please, God.*

"How are you?" he wanted to know.

"Fine," was my unemotional answer. My mind was racing: Should I tell him about my years of grief and unhappiness that followed our break up?

He asked me about my mother, my brother, and his family. I answered everything, showing neither friendliness, nor anger, nor any other emotion. I could feel myself holding back physically.

"Are you romantically involved with someone at the moment?" he wanted to know. Was this to ease his conscience, or to open a door?

"Yes. We've been together for the past thirteen years or so."

All the while there was one *big* question I had for him. *Do you have your wife's permission to call me? I have heard how possessive and terribly jealous she is.* I bit my tongue. I would not demean myself by bringing her into the conversation even though he was mentioning her name so casually as though it was the most natural thing to do, talking to me about her.

He then told me about their travels to Arizona for winters, where they could no longer go because he and his wife both have macular degeneration and cannot drive the distance. His wife did not want to travel by plane.

I was sad for his eyesight, but really not sorry that he had to obey a demanding wife. It had been his choice.

We hung up after about ten minutes.

I stood there, paralyzed, my head reeling. Was I glad? Was I angry?

Suddenly the years melted away and I was transported to the 1970s. All the emotions, the love we had shared for four years, the dancing, the dinners, the life we'd had, reappeared, and I remembered how I had been the happiest woman on Earth.

The rest of the afternoon and most of the following week I spent returning to the years 1971 through 1974, starting with our meeting during one of Rochester's worst snowstorms on February 13, 1971.

My first impression of him had not been impressive. He looked a lot older than his fifty-one years. His face was lined with deep wrinkles, and he had a tired look even though he was smiling as I sat in the front seat of his Thunderbird.

Malley, one of the senior proofreaders at work, had arranged for the blind date. Fifty-one years old, a very recent widower, and six feet tall, she'd said. I was uncomfortable about his height even though in those days I managed to add a bit to my four-feet-nine-inches through high heels and a bouffant hairdo. Fifty-one sounded so old to my thirty-seven. But Malley reassured me he was a nice guy—a coworker of the gentleman she was dating at the time.

Malley, her date, and Bob picked me up that Saturday about 6:00 p.m. while the storm was raging with a fury. I was introduced to Bob, then I sat in the front seat, since he was driving, and Malley and her date occupied the back seat. We were to go to Malley's house in Irondequoit for drinks, and from there to Rund's Restaurant on West Henrietta Road. Bob took the recently built Route 104 but took the wrong exit, veering towards Webster. Everyone was giving opinions and directions. He finally took the next exit and, reversing his route, got us to Malley's house.

The snow was still coming down hard. While we were having drinks, we wondered if the restaurant was even open. "We are open and serving dinner," was the answer when Malley telephoned. So around 7:30 we piled into Bob's car again but he drove only as far as the end of the street. The snow was so high under his car that the wheels could not touch the ground and had no traction. We were stuck. With the help of some passers-by the men pushed the car back into the driveway and we now had to make the best of a very uncomfortable situation. We had to spend the night at Malley's house.

I called my Mother to let her know I was to stay at Malley's because of the storm and not to worry; Bob called his son, Bob Jr., so he wouldn't worry. Awkward as the situation was, we made the best of it, playing board games, cooking spaghetti, and dancing and listening to records all night long. But Malley and Herbert were also in their fifties, and I found all the fifty-year-old companions' jokes not so funny. I wanted some young conversation.

By morning the roads had been cleared enough for Bob to drive me to my home off South Avenue close to Highland Hospital. This time I directed him through the shortest and simplest route. No expressways! The apartment complex had not been cleared yet and I was up to my chest in snow. Bob helped me walk towards my building.

The following week back at work Malley asked me if I had liked my date. "Because," she said, "if you liked him I will arrange for another evening out. In any case, he still owes you a dinner."

Well, he hadn't impressed me all that much, but I gave him another try. We had another date two weeks later. The four of us went to Rund's and this time there was no snow and we enjoyed ourselves.

It was during that second date when I realized that this man was really not so old. He was intelligent, I enjoyed his conversation, and he acted like the gentleman he was. That was the night I started to warm up to him.

Bob and I continued seeing each other again and again and the next thing I knew, we'd spent almost four very happy years together. The smile never left my face. We became a team, a couple. He fit into my family beautifully, and as I got to know his friends and family, I was accepted with open arms.

Whenever he came to pick me up I would be on the phone, sitting on the couch facing the front windows from where I could see him arriving. He used to joke that I must have been born with a telephone attached to my ear. When he came in, first he would greet Mother and me, have some small conversation, then we would leave. When we got in his car, he would greet me again, this time with a kiss. We saw each other four or five times a week. During the week we would go shopping for new clothes for him, or he would have dinner with us. Saturday nights we would go to a restaurant with live music and we danced the night away.

Some Sundays we would go on a picnic, just the two of us, at Durand Eastman Park. Soon I met his two sons. Bob was surprised and pleased that I was able to become so friendly with them, especially Jim, the younger one.

During the week of my fortieth birthday, Mary, my best friend from my German high school days, came to visit me from Germany so we could celebrate my birthday together. We had a wonderful time the three of us, going to dinners, dancing, and celebrating my birthday at the revolving Skylon Tower Restaurant in Niagara Falls, Canada. At the tower gift shop Mary bought me a Hummel figurine—The Chimney Sweep—for good luck. Bob also bought me a pair of Hummel figurines—a little girl and little boy on their knees, saying their prayers.

During the second year of our relationship, Bob started telling me about a neighbor family of his. The husband was very ill and their two sons were always in trouble with the law. He felt sorry for them. Bob Jr., a social worker, helped them. When the husband passed away, Bob tried to be helpful to the new widow, who wasted no time in clinging to him and letting him know that she had been attracted to him the first time she had seen him. That was while her husband was still alive. What a boost to a man's ego!

He used to tell me about the clinging widow, asking me for advice as to how to get rid of her. My answer was to not accept her invitations to dinner even though Bob Jr. was also invited. "Let Bobbie go alone, don't go with him. You are really encouraging her by trying to be polite."

I did not know how determined this woman was until one evening in the summer of 1974 Bob said to me, "I guess we should get engaged so that I can convince this woman that you come first."

I still remember the panic that hit my heart and the disappointment that our engagement could not be any more romantic than this.

"We'll get engaged because we love each other, and not because you want to send a message to that woman who has so little pride she is throwing herself at you even though she knows about me."

We continued our life as before, yet at times I sensed a difference in him.

It was on Christmas Day 1974 when my whole world came crashing down on my head and around my shoulders. He had told me that Bob Jr. was going into the seminary to study for the priesthood. This was the last year Bob would spend Christmas with his father and his son together. That's why he was not going to be able to be with me and my family that day. He came to see me that morning and brought me my present—a traveling cosmetics suitcase I had wanted. I had a sweater for him. We sat in the kitchen and he held me and cried.

Mother and I went to my brother's home for dinner as we always did for Christmas. After two glasses of champagne, I started feeling very emotional remembering Bob's tears. I called his father's house to talk with him and make him feel better. His father said Bob had been there in the morning and was not expected to come again. Next, I called his younger brother's house, thinking I had misunderstood him. His sister-in-law said they had not planned to get together that day. At this point I knew exactly where he was.

I looked up her telephone number in the telephone directory and called the woman. A young male voice answered, probably one of her sons. I simply said, "I want to talk to Bob, please."

"One moment," and Bob came to the phone.

"You lied to me," was all I could say. I could hear the shock and guilt in his voice trying to answer me. I simply hung up the phone.

All my happiness, my unending smile, vanished, and I felt betrayed by him and by life. My four happy years were no longer a reality.

But life goes on. And the years rolled by, twenty-eight of them, all the time I believing that those four years had not been real.

Then he called.

It gave me a devilish mean pleasure to hear him tell me that he had been thinking about me throughout the years. And when he hung up, using his special nickname for me, I knew for sure he regretted his marriage.

It was several weeks later when I finally realized that the phone call gave me back my four happy years. I'd had the opportunity to experience immeasurable joy. They were real.

Diagnosis:
Guillain-Barré Syndrome

Is it a syndrome or a sentence that will forever change—no, end—the active and healthy life I have known so far? I do not know much about the syndrome, only that it is debilitating. How it is contracted and how extensive the long-term problems can be are unknown to me. I therefore am expecting the worst.

The doctors are nodding their heads and explaining that all the symptoms I am exhibiting are clues to the diagnosis. In order to confirm it, I must have a spinal tap and a nerve conduction test (electromyogram, or EMG). Also, I am to be transferred to the medical intensive care unit (MICU) as soon as a bed is available. (In the midst of all this, I cannot help but notice that new initials, MICU, are used instead of just plain old ICU.)

My brother, Ohannes, and my niece Patti have been called in and they are present during this communication and commotion.

I am in shock! I want to cry! I want to run away from here! I want Marcel, my longtime life partner, who passed away one year ago. But most of all I am frightened.

This cannot be real. It is a dream—actually a nightmare. Everything around me—the walls, the people, the furniture, the noise from the hallways—seems surreal. Yet I try not to be emotional. I look at my relatives and see that Patti is trying not to show emotion on her face. Since she is a nurse, she is used to keeping a neutral expression. I know that her brain is in a state of shock like mine. My brother's face is showing emotion, his eyes are filled up, but he is also trying to appear matter of fact.

In order not to cry or scream, and also to learn more about Guillain-Barré Syndrome, I try to be logical and start asking questions about the prognosis, extent of possible rehabilitation, etc. Not knowing what the syndrome is makes it hard for me to ask the right or pertinent questions. The neurologist, Dr. Chad Heatwole, answers everything carefully and honestly. I believe him, and attempt to remember, however unsuccessfully, everything he is telling us.

There are two people inside me. One is so frightened that she is unable to accept the reality and immensity of the news. The other is calm and suppressing any display of emotion, in order not to let my family know the real pain and fear inside me.

I don't remember how much later it was when my brother and Patti had to leave. Since the doctors and assistants and the whole entourage had left also, I am all alone in the narrow, uncomfortable emergency department bed.

There is a curtain in the middle of the room separating two patients to give each some privacy. The other patient, also a woman, has two people sitting with her. They may be relatives or friends, I do not know and I do not care. At least they do not bother me, because even though they are talking, they are not loud. There is constant commotion in the hallway and I see people in white vests, walking in and out of the pharmacy just across from my cubicle.

I have to wait for the tests. I try not to think of the spinal tap. I try not to frighten myself. After all, if I stay calm, what will be will be. I tell myself, just don't think of the pain! The treatment, called plasmapheresis or plasma exchange, has a success rate of 80 percent, I have been told. I worry; what if I am within the 20 percent?

I pick up the telephone next to me and call Sato, my Armenian friend from Egypt, about every five minutes, but I can hardly talk. My mouth is dry, and the paralysis on the left side of my face makes it difficult to formulate words clearly.

Panic engulfs me. I need someone to be with me and to hold my hand, to give me comfort and support. I have read about people having a panoramic view of their whole life. Mine goes forward into the future—a future that is a dark tunnel. I am in a wheelchair, helpless and useless. What will my friends and family think of me? The me who had always been present, dependable, helpful to friends and family. I am not afraid of dying. What I am afraid of is not being able to be me again.

How did I get here?

It started in the middle of May. I was feeling pretty well, looking forward to a wonderful spring after arthroscopic surgery on my right knee in April. I was making plans to start a serious regimen of walking and other fun exercises offered at Perinton Community Center. I even tried a class of line dancing one Saturday, thinking it should be a breeze! But my feet just did not follow the orders given by my brain.

I was disappointed that I had lost the agility of my younger days, and thought it was because of my knee surgery, unaware that it was the beginning of this syndrome.

For about two weeks I noticed other strange symptoms:

My toes tingled all the time. In bed at night, my feet felt as though I was wearing socks. I kept trying to remove them by rubbing my feet against the sheets. But of course I *knew* there were no socks on my feet!

My fingers tingled constantly. I kept rubbing my hands together as often as I could, but with no relief.

Water from the faucet felt icy on my hands. When I drank the water, it was normal room temperature.

One day, when I touched my stomach, I had no feeling. I kept rubbing it over and over again, but there was still no feeling.

I felt achy all over, and I was beginning to stumble when

walking.

It did occur to me that these were very strange occurrences.

Then one day I had an intense and unbearable pain in my back. I was in agony. I made an emergency appointment with my doctor. Dr. Mala Gupta examined me and, since I only complained of my back pain, she prescribed a muscle relaxant because she said my back was tense. Had I told her of the other physical phenomena, she might have had a clue of what was really going on.

I took the medicine but it did not help and the back pain got worse.

A few days later, I arose early in the morning to go to the doctor's office again. By now I was stumbling so much that I started using the walker I had got for Marcel.

I went to the bathroom with the portable telephone in my hand. I closed the door, put the telephone on the vanity, and as I tried to bend, my left knee buckled and I fell forward. As I was falling, a voice in my head was saying, "Okay, here we go." And I let myself fall.

I tried to get up but I couldn't. I tried to lift myself into a sitting position, and again I couldn't. I looked up and found that the doorknob was too high to reach. I kept thinking, "If I don't panic, I will find a way to get out." I kept trying to sit up, over and over again, and each time I failed.

At one point, I did get into a sitting position, but when I

reached for the doorknob, I fell back again. My arms and legs had become so weak I could not use them to lift myself up. I waited for pain but I had none. Good, at least there were no broken bones.

What to do? "I shall not stay here. There is a solution. I must not panic." I remembered the telephone on the vanity, but it was out of reach. I pulled a towel from the rod just in front of me and swung it on the vanity. After a couple of tries, the telephone fell to the floor with the towel. Aah, success! I called my brother. He arrived with my next-door neighbor who had a set of my keys. We called 911, and an ambulance transported me to the hospital.

By now, I decided to tell my strange symptoms to the emergency room staff who surrounded me and kept asking all kinds of questions. They looked at me with blank stares. They wanted to make sure I had not broken any bones as a result of the fall. I was not complaining of any pain other than in my back, which had started about two weeks before the fall.

Since they had no diagnosis for the back pain and the difficulty in walking, I was discharged the following day and sent to a nursing home for rehabilitation and physical therapy for my "weak legs." No one explained to me why I had those weak legs.

My symptoms got worse. I never received the physical therapy, since I had arrived at the nursing home at 8:00 p.m.

on a Friday and the offices were closed for the weekend. I had to wait until Monday to start the therapy. By Saturday, even the walker was not enough to assist me, and by evening I was in a wheelchair.

On Sunday, the left side of my face drooped and I had difficulty speaking clearly. A head nurse and, to my knowledge, one other nurse were the only medical personnel on the premises. The physician's assistant for the nursing home was called in. She thought I might have Bell's palsy and reassured me that it was not a stroke. She nonetheless listened to me carefully when I told her of my strange symptoms.

On Monday morning, I went to the physical therapy room, looking forward to getting some help. The therapists were concerned about my physical condition. They decided that I should be sent to the emergency department at Strong Memorial Hospital again. I was diagnosed with Bell's palsy and thrush, and sent back to the nursing home.

By now my emotional state had become extremely tense. I could not do anything by myself. I needed help each time I got in and out of bed. My back pain was so intense that I could neither lie down nor sit up comfortably. I called the nurse about ten times each night to help me get in and out of my bed to see if I could get some relief.

I could not eat my meals in the dining room. The wheelchair was too low for me to reach the table comfortably. Also, because of my paralyzed face, I could not eat anything without some or most of it spilling out of my mouth. Drinking was not easy either, since the fluid spilled out also. While chewing my food, I kept biting my tongue and lips and the inside of my cheeks. I had no feeling on the left side of my face. So I stayed in my room during meal times.

On Tuesday morning, I was wheeled to the therapy room again. I had hardly started on one exercise when the social worker came in and told me that the doctor wanted me back in the hospital. I thought, what doctor is it? I never found out. The ambulance had already been called and was at the door. My niece had also been called and was at the hospital. Someone along the way—I don't know who—had listened to my symptoms seriously. When I arrived at the hospital, the staff from Neurology surrounded me and the final diagnosis of Guillain-Barré syndrome was established.

What I lived through was a miracle, with a staff of four different departments taking good care of me with patience. The days and nights blended together. Every other day, during the first ten days, I was wheeled to the Aphaeresis department for my plasma exchange.

The attention and care was impeccable. In addition to the medical treatments, several people—the doctor, the nurse, and the physical therapist—patiently listened to me. I cried as I told my life story in half an hour, or else I tried to be unnaturally jovial. I was in a state of what felt like a twilight zone. I slept all the time, while still aware of my surroundings, wondering if I was in another dimension of existence.

One of the doctors at MICU asked a former Guillain-Barré Syndrome (GBS) patient to please come and talk to me about her experiences. During my second treatment, as I lay with the tubes attached to my throat and the machines whirling my blood through the necessary cycles, a smiling pretty lady in her early seventies walked in.

She was impeccably dressed and had a box of fresh strawberries from her husband's garden. Juanice (Marcella) Morgan sat with me during the whole hour and told me about her experience. There was one difference, though. She had been so far gone and it had happened so quickly that she had been in a coma for several days and had been put on a ventilator. She therefore had no recollection of the plasma exchange when it was performed on her.

Seeing and hearing her gave me the courage to look patiently forward to my healing. Juanice later visited me a few more times and brought me more strawberries, and flowers too.

Juanice Morgan was not the only visitor. My friends, family, and even former coworkers arrived and brought me their support. They visited me, sent cards and flowers, and in every way let me know how much I was loved and respected. I am so very grateful to everyone.

Day by day I learned to adapt to my disabilities in the following ways:

I learned how to use a straw to drink liquids from the good side of my mouth.

The hospital kitchen sent all my food pureed so I did not have to chew and bite my tongue and/or my upper lip.

Blowing my nose and brushing my teeth became experiences in creativity.

Daily physical and occupational therapy helped improve and strengthen my legs, arms, and fingers.

My mother had spent her seventy-fifth birthday at the hospital during a heart emergency. In a few more weeks I was to turn seventy-five years of age, and I could not help making the comparison and, feeling guilty, hoped to be home by my birthday. Miraculously I was, just days before the big day!

By mid-October I continued to improve at a slower pace, and I now notice the changes by the month instead of by the week. Just as the syndrome started from the extremities toward the center of my body (from toes and fingers toward the middle of me), the healing started gradually from the center of my body back outwards.

I am grateful that I can walk on my own. I rely on a walker only when I am outside my home, or when first standing up after having sat for a while. I am even more grateful that I can drive my car. Family and friends have been so very helpful in giving me rides to doctors' appointments or to go shopping. But the independence of driving on one's own is priceless.

I still have problems that may never go away. But they do not hinder me from having a normal life.

Yes, I am seventy-five years old. Before this syndrome hit me, I had never considered myself old. I always thought of myself as a young person. When I was at the hospital, suddenly the years rolled by almost overnight. I seemed to have aged suddenly.

But then, something changed in me. A state of calm settled itself inside me, and in spite of the "aging" I have undergone, I came to accept myself for who and what I have become. If anyone thinks I am making a big deal out of my age, well, yes. It is a Big Deal!

I am alive, but also I feel I am removed from life. I feel that I am in the world, but I am looking at it from the outside. I seem to be gliding through my days mostly in calmness and peace. I like it!

I do not know what else life has in store for me or how much longer I have to live. As soon as I have regained the full use of my hands and fingers, I shall get into an active life as much as I can. I shall go for my walks. I shall learn line dancing. I shall do volunteer work wherever I can be of assistance. For now, I am aiming at resuming everything in the spring or summer of 2009.

Postscript

Today, at the time of this printing (2017), I have recovered almost 95 percent. I am self-sufficient and live on my own. I exhibit hardly any symptoms. Anyone who does not know of my having had GBS cannot discern any disability

Even though my walk is a little stiff and there are some minor difficulties, my most debilitating problem is the sudden draining of energy. I have heard of this problem from most of the former patients with whom I have come in contact.

Life goes on, and I go on.

An Experience in the Snow

In Egypt the only snow we had seen was either in textbooks or magazines, on Christmas greeting cards, and in movies. In Alexandria winter was cold, rainy, and damp. As for Cairo, rains were rare but welcome occasions. Now I live with snow just about six months of each year.

The first time I saw snow was at the age of twenty-three in Lebanon where I had gone in February of 1957 to study at Haigazian College in Beirut. Between semesters the student council had organized a day trip to the mountains. Since I had just arrived to start during the second semester, I was invited to join them to get acquainted with my classmates. Everyone was dressed appropriately with boots, heavy coats, and winter gloves. Some were planning on skiing. I had my winter coat and my favorite red shoes on. It was a glorious and sunny winter day. We all piled into the bus, which drove us to one of the mountain ski resorts. As we all started to climb a snow-covered hill, in addition to getting freezing feet, I ruined the shoes. "Oh well!" I thought. I don't know what I had expected, but I kept picking up fistfuls of snow, looking at it in detail, expecting to find those beautiful hexagonal crystals I had seen in pictures. It was just white fluff—no beautiful six-sided lacy designs! I then put some in my mouth expecting a new taste; it was a new texture and at the same time it was bland—just frozen water!

Since I've been in Rochester some fifty years now, my opinion of snow is no longer that of wonderment even though I always look forward to its first arrival. I love to wake up in the morning and watch out of my window to see that first white, pure fluff. Through the years I've watched snow falling gently, in a blizzard, or simply as flurries. I have walked in it and driven in it while it was already on the ground or as it was falling, gently and otherwise! Through the years I have also had many interesting experiences because of snow, one of which I'd like to share here:

On December 30, 1987, I was driving to work from Brighton to Webster. As I had always joked, this day I was on the road before the snow trucks, at about 6:00 a.m. I was on Penfield Road, driving toward Panorama Plaza. It had snowed the night before, so I was being cautious as I started the downhill part. Suddenly my car skidded, veered to the left, and ended up in the ditch. I sat there for a moment collecting myself and thinking how best I could slowly pull out of there when a red station wagon appeared out of nowhere and parked next to my car.

A big man got out, came towards my car, and as I lowered the window, he told me, "You better get out of here fast. The snow trucks will be coming soon."

"That's what I'm trying to do," I stammered.

"Get over to the passenger side, I'll drive you out."

I don't know why I was not afraid of him. He took the driver's seat and gently backed the car to the right lane on the road.

As he was getting out, he said, "You'll be all right now. Just drive and trust your car."

I thanked him and started driving, trying to stay calm and to "trust my car." At the same time, I tried to see what kind of station wagon the man had, wanting to read some writing that was on one door. But he had already gone. In somewhat of a daze, I continued on to my destination on Publishers Parkway. I drove into the parking lot of The Lawyers Co-operative Publishing Company, Manufacturing Division, and parked the car in the first open spot I saw. As I was getting out of my car, I noticed a pair of men's winter gloves on the passenger seat. They looked brand new. I sadly thought that they probably were a Christmas present from a dear person and my angel in the snow had forgotten them in my car while helping me.

I wanted to return them to their owner. But when I started asking questions of several coworkers who were volunteer firefighters, describing to them the red vehicle I had seen, no one recognized it. Sadly, I could do nothing.

I kept the gloves for several years, with hopes of some day

finding their owner. They sat in my attic on top of a pile of blankets, the brown suede gloves lined with fur. Each time I looked at them I remembered the kindness of the stranger.

Finally, in 1999 when I was getting rid of most of the contents of my four-bedroom Cape Cod house in order to be able to fit into a two-bedroom condominium, I donated the gloves to a charity. I couldn't help thinking that the magical man who had helped me to safety in the snow now would be helping a poor homeless man to stay warm.

Was my helper really an angel in the snow?

My Best Friend

My friend sits quietly, listening to me whenever I need to talk, never uttering a criticism. My friend doesn't even give me advice. With a serious and kind expression, my friend keeps staring ahead as though it knows some deep secret and will never tell of it. It gives me the impression that it knows my future, the good and the bad, and is waiting to see what my reaction will be as life events develop. It is almost as though it is with me just to give me support along the way I will inevitably go.

My friend has no name. From the very beginning, it never occurred to me to give it one. I love it, it is mine, and that's all that ever mattered.

Let me tell you about our first meeting as told to me by my mother.

When I was one year old, back in Alexandria, I got an infection in my eyes. They were filled with pus and I kept them shut tightly. No matter how hard they tried, my parents could not use drops or ointment prescribed by the doctor, because I would not let anyone touch my eyes. My parents were desperate and the doctor had warned them that if they did not get me to open my eyes to let the infection out, I would lose my eyesight.

Eby and Kiki tried to entice me by bringing me items I loved so that I would open my eyes to look at them. "Look, what is this?" my parents would ask, hoping that I would want to look at it. Nothing doing! "Look at Mimi (one of my dolls), she wants you to see her new dress. Look, Dédé brought your favorite Nestlé chocolates, and if you want to have some, you have to open your eyes to unwrap them." I would touch the items or toy or chocolates, and name them, all the while keeping my eyes shut tight.

One day my Father brought me an item I could not recognize. It was sort of hard and wrapped in cellophane paper, something I had no way of recognizing. After touching it from all angles, I was puzzled. I kept asking, "What is it?" But all they answered was, "If you want to know what it is, you have to look at it." I opened my eyes to see it. Blood and pus gushed out of my eyes. Immediately Mother cleaned my face and was able to put in the drops the doctor had prescribed. The infection gradually cleared and my eyesight was saved.

This magical object had no special meaning to a one-year-old at the time. But it was always treated gently by the family and considered mine. It gradually became my favorite possession.

It is truly amazing that it did not get damaged during World War II as had most of our possessions, including our home.

It traveled to Cairo with us during the war and then back to Alexandria. It traveled with me during my student days to Beirut and sat on the bookshelf above the desk. And when I came to the United States, I brought my best friend with me. Now it sits on the dresser in my bedroom making sure that I am still okay.

My best friend is a ceramic dog, and I think of it as my Seeing Eye Dog. It is beige, has a black nose, one black ear, a black spot at the tip of the other ear, and another black mark on its back. There is a hole at the bottom because it is hollow, and at the time when Father bought it, it was filled with candy.

Through the years I have played with it, stroked and hugged it like a stuffed toy, and I remember the day I wrote my name at the bottom in Armenian to make sure that everyone knew it belongs to me:

Պերճուհի

As it sits on my dresser, I do pick it up periodically and stroke it with a smile. I wonder what special blessing kept it alive all these years. I talk to it sometimes and ask questions when I need someone (or something) to help me with a decision. It is amazing that at my age I still have this love for it and miraculously it is still with me when so much else has been lost.

In recent years I have developed glaucoma, which is under

constant and vigilant care of my ophthalmologist. I know it has progressed but only time will tell as to how far it will go. My friend saved my eyesight once, and I am sure it is still watching over me to keep my eyes as healthy as possible, for as long as possible. But time is running short and this condition is advancing. I do hope my friend will be available for me to hold and stroke and know its identity if I live long enough and actually reach the point of losing my eyesight.

DETACHMENT

At eighty I seem to be on the threshold of a new beginning. I feel there is a door opening for newer experiences. Though my body is aging and my mind is losing its original sharpness, I am desperate to feel as alive as always.

I am in the process of making a major, and I hope final, life-changing transition that requires selling my present home. To downsize, I have to let go of so many items I treasure.

Yet, how can I detach myself from any piece without the risk of forgetting the person who gave it to me or who helped me create the memory? How can I detach myself from the dark red counted-cross-stitch runner Mother had made especially for me? It resembles a piece of Persian carpet and I have had it framed with a border of metallic fringe bought in Beirut in 1963 before I came to the US. It now hangs on the wall above the sofa.

How about the wool bed jacket my grandmother, my Néné, had knitted for me just before I left Egypt for the last time, which I have kept all these years, my favorite blue and white item, but which I never wore because I am allergic to wool?

156

Every time I touch it or see it hanging in my closet I remember my Néné and then, strangely, the tomato plants in her garden in Alexandria come to mind. I actually smell them.

Shall I name a few more? Here goes:

There is my christening dress, which Mother had made and embroidered, and which brings me the vision of the young woman who created it with all her love for her little baby girl. The first baby she ever kissed, she once told me.

Then there is the exquisitely detailed four-inch-high bronze sailboat Father had made from a cast—one for our home, one for Uncle Garo, and one for Aunt Vartoug. When Mother came to the United States, she brought ours with her and gave it to my brother. After Uncle Garo passed away, I asked Vartoug, who used to visit us often, to bring his boat to me. Garo had become a widower and had no children. It now sits on my desk and has double its value in sentiment. Father had made it, and it came from Garo's home. How do I part with this?

Yesterday I took down the cardboard box I keep in one corner of the shelf in my closet. It is marked *Memories* in my handwriting. I opened it to examine the contents. There were a few pictures from high school days, every single one of Lawyers Co-operative Publishing Company's news magazines in which I had been mentioned for some accomplishment as an employee, my nameplate from my desk.

I remind myself that throughout life people lose possessions just as dear to them because of fires, hurricanes, floods, wars, and any number of other disasters. I think of Mother, who had to get rid of everything we owned in Alexandria before coming to Rochester to be with us. How did she do it? Maybe the hope and anticipation of being reunited with her children helped in her detachments. She also gave many pieces to her family members in addition to donations to charity.

Mother did it, and so shall I. I look forward to living in a whole new environment that will be certainly neater and simpler, giving me more time to enjoy my new life where my responsibilities for my home will be lighter. I am promised new experiences of socializing, attending lectures, concerts, dinners, and the other joys life can bring to my last few years. I am hoping that my health will cooperate and not create too many problems.

Tomorrow I'll open the box again, touch each item with feeling and emotion, and make a decision to keep it or not.

There will always be just a few, such as I have mentioned above, that shall remain with me until the day I die. Others I can more easily be rid of. I shall pass as many as possible to my nieces and nephew and dear friends, hoping that they will find as much joy in them as I did, and I'll take only the closest memories with me to my new home at Brickstone of St. John's.

But Where Is the Real She?

As the years go by, we become more reflective of our pasts. Now that we have retired from active work, no longer have teenagers to taxi around to their various activities, and are not in charge of major dinner parties for the holidays (the younger generations we taxied around a while back are taking over), we have more time for memories and philosophizing.

We often remember friends and family members who have made their impressions on our lives and now have gone to their resting places, wherever those may be—nursing homes if still living, or heaven, we hope, if no longer with us. We smile, we shed a few tears, and overall we have a warm feeling for having had them in our lives. We certainly miss them and sometimes see them in our dreams. Even though memory does play tricks with us, embellishing or minimizing long-ago happenings, we still have most of the memories.

But what about the friend or relative who is still with us and has been taken over by dementia or Alzheimer's? What about his or her memories? What about our friendship or relationship?

My closest friend, the one I have had since we were nineteen, has succumbed to this thief. She is here physically, but where is the real she?

I met Anahid immediately after I finished my German School years in the fall of 1952. Because I was planning to continue my studies at an English language university, my parents enrolled me at the Scottish School for Girls in Alexandria so I could improve my English language skills. Anahid was one of my classmates there. We hit it off right away. The class was made up of about thirty girls of various backgrounds: Armenian, Greek, Italian, Jewish, Lebanese-Syrian, and even one English girl. It turned out that Anahid and I lived very close, separated by only a couple of houses. This was perfect for taking the tram and walking the rest of the way to and from school together.

The following year Anahid got engaged and then married a thirty-six-year-old widower with two young daughters.

Following the 1956 Suez Crisis, I went to Beirut, Lebanon, to study at the then Beirut College for Women. There was no e-mail and no Skype in those days: we corresponded the old-fashioned way, through letters home to friends and relatives.

Anahid's mother passed away unexpectedly that year. Anahid used to visit my mother often even though I was not there. She wrote to me one day asking if I would mind it if she and my mother adopted each other. She put it this way: "I need a mother and your mother needs a daughter. We are both lonely. I hope you won't mind."

Mind? I was delighted. This would lessen the constant worry I had about the loneliness I had caused my mother by studying abroad. She was not alone; Father was still alive then and she had her family, but her family was in Cairo and in communication through letters only and occasional visits for special occasions.

Anahid and I would visit and enjoy time together during my trips home for summers and holidays. In 1960, I got my degree and went home. I started teaching English in Cairo at the American College for Girls, leaving my mother alone again, but I often spent weekends in Alexandria.

The next big event was the birth of Anahid's son, Ara, in March 1961.

In 1962 I returned to Beirut to continue my studies, this time at the famous American University of Beirut, and Anahid and her family—husband, two daughters, and son—emigrated to Canada. The following year, 1963, I came to the US.

As soon as I came to Rochester, Anahid came to visit me with her now four-year-old son.

As time and life continued, I bought a car, then Mother came to join us and lived with me for the rest of her life. All the while Anahid and I were in constant communication. Sundays were our long-distance calling days. At any given opportunity, Mother and I would drive to Toronto to visit her and her family. Sometimes Mother would stay with her for a few days until I went back to get her. Whenever Mother was in the hospital,

Anahid would come to visit her and stay with me for a few days. The years rolled by. Her daughters each made their own lives and her son became a pharmacist. Unfortunately, he developed a rare form of cancer and passed away in his early forties.

I still call her as often as I can. During her son's illness the calls were daily. When her husband was admitted into the nursing home, she'd call me at any time of the day or night crying and afraid of being by herself in a large house. Her daughters moved her to a condo apartment so she would feel safer. She had started the dreadful disease and it was progressing. At the time, I had no idea that what she was going through was not just grief or loneliness. She told me she'd gotten lost on the highway and it scared her. I said, "That's not hard to do in the greater Toronto area, and how many of us have not been lost at one time or another?"

I went to visit her and she was afraid of driving to the most familiar places. Eventually her daughters told me about her condition.

I go through various emotions: sometimes I try to see a glimmer of hope and tell myself that she is not so very badly lost; she still has listening and reasoning abilities. At other times I despair realizing that she really is not in her body. She has already left, or is in the process of leaving and I am talking to a shell.

Whereas in the past I used to call her on the phone every

single day, now I call her about once a week and often dread having to do it. I do not know how to make her feel happy or make her feel that she is having a normal conversation.

So far she recognizes my voice and calls me by my name as soon as I say "Hi." Yet I wonder if it is out of habit that she calls my name or whether she recognizes my voice. Every single time she asks me when I shall visit her. One of the saddest times was when she wondered how far I lived. She said, "Are you still in the same place?" I have no idea what place she referred to. Rochester? Alexandria?

I don't know what she really meant. I know that she tries to cover up the extent of her forgetting and is actually afraid. I pacify her and say I shall be visiting Toronto soon.

Then she wants to know what I did today. I come up with some trivial activity like going shopping or going to the doctor. Then she goes through telling me where she lives (by now, the nursing home) with her husband (they have rooms next to each other), and that there are some people there and they take good care of her. She does not leave the building, she tells me, and then asks me what I did today, and when am I going to visit her.

I shall always be grateful to her daughter Sonia who drove her to Rochester for a couple of days so we could be with each other a couple of years ago. I was very happy and she was happy. I saw the extent of the disease's ravage. She was confused and didn't seem to be sure of anything. Everything around her was

1966. Toronto at Anahid's house.

unfamiliar to her even though she had been in my new condo several times in happier days. Even so, she still tried to be "normal." She smiled, hugged me, and felt happy to be with me, but always with an expression of some confusion and hesitation.

I have agonized over her so much, wanting to help her but unable to do so. I think of her every single day trying to cover the picture of the new Anahid with the former one, the one that was the closest thing I had to a dear sister who loved me back and trusted me with her soul.

Having dealt with her, I have come to the conclusion that people with this terrible disease appear normal though they are ill and whatever you do to make them happy is worth it because they are living in the moment and the moment is what counts. If you can make them happy for just a few moments, it's worth it; that's all you can hope for. Nothing long term, no tomorrow, no yesterday, because memory is unknown.

Eventually, the day came when they took away her telephone and we truly lost each other.

And then one morning, Sonia called me to let me know that her mother had passed away the night before. I had been praying for this news. She is at peace now. And I miss her very much.

LETTER TO EBY

Before I start the letter, let me tell my reader who Eby is, or was: she was my mother and Eby is not her full name. As a child I used to call her by that name because I could not say Ebrouhi. I also called my father Kiki, my own version of Krikor.

I have found that most first-born children will call their parents by their first name because that is what they hear from everyone around them. If no one teaches a child to call the parents Mummy or Daddy, or any other equivalent name, then that child calls them by what name everyone else is using. In our case, eventually, my brother and I used to call our mother Eby Mama because that name satisfied everyone. We of course outgrew this as the years went by.

Years later, when I went to Beirut for the last time and then came to the United States, I started my letters to her with Dear Eby, instead of Dear Mother, because it was important to keep my being here a secret from the Egyptian government. I wrote in the tone of a friend, not a daughter. I don't really know how successful this was; at least we did not advertise my being here instead of in Beirut studying.

When Mother eventually joined us here and later started her artwork, we thought using Eby was an easier name for a signature instead of Ebrouhi. Eby could stand by itself, whereas Ebrouhi needed to have the full name of Ebrouhi Esmerian.

The following is a letter I had to write to her.

January 1, 2014

Dear Eby,

It is January 1 again and I think of you and want to sit and write you a letter like I used to when I was in Beirut, and later in the US, and we communicated by letters. Even though I used to write to you at least once, and often twice, a week, I always started the New Year with a letter to you.

Those were the days when no one had heard of e-mails, cell phones, and all the other social media communications of today. That's when the arrival of the mail was a happy experience—it brought your letters and those of other relatives and friends I missed. To this day the mail carrier is one of my favorite people even though now he or she brings bills to pay and hardly any letters "from home."

I loved to go to the stationery store and buy pretty letter paper of various sizes and for various purposes. Some people used aerograms they purchased from the Post Office because it was less expensive, since it was just the cost of the stamp; but not me—I had to have the fancy paper to write on.

After you came to live with me here in Rochester, I still kept writing my letter on January 1, but this time it was to your sister in Cairo and to my dearest friend Anahid in Toronto. You have been gone for twenty-five years now and if I no longer think of you every single day, I still write you a letter in my mind on January 1 every single year. And I still miss you and look for your quiet, constant wisdom that you gave me when I needed it.

Your loving daughter,

Berdjoug
(the shortened version of my name)

2017

It is New Year's Day today.

It is a worldwide holiday. The beginning of a new cycle when we all look forward to it being better than the year before. Even when the year before had been a good one, we look forward to a still better year. As for every beginning, we put our efforts and prayers for this new year to be good for our health, relationships, families, friends, and to bring us a peaceful world (yeah, what a dream . . .). Yes, we look forward.

As far back as I can remember, I have always looked forward with optimism toward the daily progress of each new year. January first always gave me a feeling of a new start.

Just as always, I woke up this first morning a little later than my usual time, having stayed up to greet 2017 at midnight. I got out of bed and realized that I was somewhat blank inside. I continued my routine morning activities and eventually got in my car and went to do some grocery shopping, all the while as unemotional as I had started the day. I was not happy, I was not sad. It was a strange non-feeling. I decided that this was sort of a dread of the unknown future of the new era that will be upon us in just three weeks. But that did not make sense; every day is an unknown, always. As I continued to be under this strange non-emotion, I continued driving. Traffic was light and the parking lot at Wegmans not crowded. As I parked my car I noticed that a previous shopper had left a shopping cart close to my parking spot. Very gladly I grabbed it and went inside—I didn't need to carry my cane while I used a cart.

After finishing my shopping, I looked for a checkout reserved for handicapped customers because the register is lower than the regular checkouts and it suits me perfectly. I don't have to stand on tiptoe to see the screen on the register and sign my name. I can actually look down. These lanes are usually crowded by non-handicapped customers who have a huge number of items in their carts. I still like them because I am in no hurry. There were two people before me. The cashier was working with the first one and the second person was emptying his cart on the conveyor belt. He was a tall, middle-aged man who looked to be in a bad mood (just like me?). He was emptying his cart by throwing the items on the conveyor without caring how they fell, looking neither to the right nor to the left.

I thought, "What a grouch. Chances are he will not even bother to put the separator stick after he's done." And I waited to be right in my conclusion. Suddenly a very faint voice in my chest told me (yes, I actually heard it) that he was acting gruff most probably because he had a problem. His face showed no emotion. I told myself, "Don't jump to conclusions. This may be a person who has an illness. He does look like he is shopping for himself and maybe he has recently lost his wife or life partner, or maybe he celebrated too much last night." I started to look at the magazines and candy that are always at checkouts and patiently waited my turn.

After he finished emptying his cart, as the belt moved forward and some space opened up, the gentleman ahead of me leaned over, picked up a separator stick, and placed it after his items.

As he turned to me and gave me a hint of a smile, he bent down and took the double-sized Cheerios from the bottom level of my cart and lifted it onto the conveyor belt for me. And then he said, "You like your Cheerios, don't you?"

I answered, "The large box promised to be cheaper." There was no other conversation. He finished his payment and went off, all the time without any kind of expression on his face other than seeming to be in a bad mood. I was glad I had been wrong about his being a grouch. He turned out to be a decent guy.

Then the cashier asked the usual "How are you today?" and I answered my usual "I am fine, and how about you?"

"I am fine, so far" was her reply. I smiled at her response as I realized that she had quite a sense of humor and I commented that she was smart, then added something to the effect of who knows what the next moment will bring.

After I had paid for my items and was wheeling my cart out of the line, I put my gloves and my sunglasses on—it was a sunny day—and proceeded to my car.

I do love my car because it has all-wheel drive and gives me the feeling that as I am driving, and especially turning corners, we meld together. But it is not the most practical one for me. I bought it in too much of a haste and did not check out certain things to see if we belonged together in practical ways. The trunk door opens too high and I have great difficulty reaching up and closing it again. And no, it cannot be refitted with something or other to make it convenient for my size. I simply have to live with it. I opened the trunk, placed my items in it, and as I turned around to close the trunk door, a woman walked up to me and said she'd be happy to take the empty cart from me and then closed my trunk door for me and said, "Happy New Year." "And to you too. Thank you for helping me," I replied.

I got in my car, and with a parking lot that was even emptier than before, I was out of there in no time.

As I drove home, I realized that my mood was changing, and it hit me that no matter what the world brings or no matter what the "new era" presents to us, the world is still full of kind and thoughtful and cheerful human beings, whether they appear so or not. And I am glad I am living in this world.

Every year is a new beginning, no matter what it brings.

PART THREE

MY
ANCESTRAL
HOMELAND

Finding Armenia

As you know by now, I was born and grew up in the beautiful city of Alexandria in Egypt within an Armenian home. We spoke Armenian in the family, and because of the cosmopolitan atmosphere and the fortunate circumstances of the era, we spoke several other languages as well. Even though we attended Armenian schools, and had a flourishing community well known and respected in our host country, I always felt that I existed but was not allowed to be officially acknowledged as an Armenian. I felt that we were the stepchildren of the world.

Those of us who lived in the Diaspora were part of the citizens of the host countries. I was a proud Egyptian and yet I often wondered if I really belonged there. In 1915 about one and a half million Armenians had been killed with the intention of annihilating us. Even though I was among the few fortunate ones whose parents had not gone through the Genocide (Father had come to Egypt before 1915 while a child of ten, and Mother was born in Alexandria), almost every Armenian we knew told a sad story of having lost every member of his or her family. Many established Armenian families had living with them one or two adopted orphans, rescued from the deserts during the "marches" or from the orphanages. This was part of our life.

Our non-Armenian neighbors, and later our classmates in non-Armenian schools, had their own separate nationalities and free countries. The Italians, the Greeks, the English, the French, the Germans, the Maltese, and, after 1948, the Jews, lived in Egypt but had their own countries they identified with. We were Armenians but also Egyptian subjects. We belonged to Egypt, even though our heritage, culture, and religion were Armenian. There was a country far away we loved very much; we had learned of its old glorious as well as tragic history in school, but we had no claim to it. It existed, and at the same time it was out of bounds, especially because it had become part of the Soviet Union after a short independence in the early 1920s.

I moved to the United States in the early 1960s and spent my entire adult life here. As far back as I can remember, I always wanted to see what Armenia was like. I wanted to be there, touch the soil under my feet, see Mount Ararat, stand on the shores of Lake Sevan with the famous fish so delicious that authors had written about. I wanted to touch the trees in the apricot orchards, the almond trees. I always wondered what Armenia was like, yet never dreamt that I would one day stand on its soil. At the age of seventy, Marcel, my life partner, gave me the miraculous opportunity to experience for myself the Armenia I had loved for so long. It was my seventieth birthday present from him.

Marcel and I, together with three other Rochester friends, started out of Rochester, New York, on Monday, September 22, 2003, and flew to Kennedy Airport. There, we proceeded to the international terminal, where the rest of the pilgrims from all over the United Sates joined us. In all we were about fifty. In the evening we took off for Vienna, Austria. From there we flew to Yerevan, the capital of Armenia, arriving at Zvartnots Airport in the early morning hours of the following day.

Exhausted, dirty, looking for rest, the first thing we met was a gray concrete tunnel out of the plane. We walked through this depressing passage toward the customs and baggage claim area. I was trying very hard not to be disappointed. I was tired from the exhausting thirty-hour trip and emotionally unprepared to deal with this first impression of bleak ugliness. The spurt of joy that jolted my heart on the airplane when the pilot welcomed the passengers in Armenian disappeared.

The customs area was disorderly, everyone pushing, trying to get ahead of everyone else. There were no lines to follow. I wondered if we would even get all of our luggage. I could see from an opening behind a desk the baggage belt going around and around, and was faintly amazed to see the same technology of processing the luggage as other countries.

Suddenly an official guided us out of the crowd and we were allowed to pass on ahead. The pilgrims were being given the privilege of going through without difficulty. Our passports were examined and stamped by an Armenian inspector and we went to get the suitcases. It did not take long to get ours, they were all there, and we went on to the bus that was waiting for us.

When we were still talking of this pilgrimage in celebration of the one thousand seven hundredth anniversary of the building of Etchmiadzin Cathedral, the Mother Church, just the thought that I was to visit Armenia, my ancestral home, brought tears to my eyes. So where were the tears now?

When the passports arrived with the visas stamped in Armenian letters, tears filled my eyes. I told myself, *What did you expect? Of course it would be in the Armenian language. It is a visa to Armenia, from the Armenian Embassy in Washington!* Just seeing that alphabet on the official documents made my heart sing. When the pilot officially welcomed the passengers to Armenia in our own language, I was smiling with tears in my eyes. So where was my song now?

I am in Armenia! I should be happy! I kept telling myself. But I was not. My heart was like a block of ice. I fought desperately not to accept the reality of the dismal, dusty, sad, gray location.

Was this really Armenia? I had expected to find poverty, some disarray, and disappointments. But this was actually crushing.

By the time we arrived at the Congress Hotel, a brand new and modern building, I was so cross and in such a bad mood that I wouldn't have wanted to be my own friend. Fortunately the room assignments went smoothly. We had room 223, *yergoo hayroor kusanuh yerek,* and were able to rest for a while in a clean and air-conditioned environment.

After a short nap, we had breakfast, then cleaned up and rested some more. My crossness gradually dissipated. In the back of my mind there was a faint emotion I might call joy. These people were speaking my mother tongue. And everyone was so pleasant and smiling: from the young women at the front desk to the bellboys, to the chambermaids. All Armenians!

In the afternoon we went for a long walk to Vernissage, a very large and famous flea market where we discovered the most beautiful and exquisite wood sculptures and artwork, and did some shopping, talking in Armenian with the vendors.

But I was still in a strange mood. I would vacillate between thinking of the Armenians as "they" or "them" and my group, the visitors, as "we." Then I would realize that we were all of the same heritage. I was Armenian, just like them. Yet there was a resistance in my heart. I was not one of them. I was an outsider Armenian.

For several days we visited various museums, the Madenataran (the main library), old churches, Holy Etchmiadzin, and the new St. Gregory the Illuminator Cathedral. At every church we lit candles. During one of our very early morning walks around the park close to the hotel, I discerned the faint silhouette of Mount Ararat and pointed it out to Marcel. This almost stirred a slight emotion in my body, but the ice froze any hint of tears.

As part of the tour we were to attend a presentation by a young dance group. We arrived in two buses and were greeted by about a dozen young girls dressed in pink, each holding flowers. As we approached, they descended the steps at the entrance to the theater and greeted us by presenting the flowers to each of us. My lips started trembling, my eyes got wet.

We went through the building into the theater itself, where several rows of seats had been reserved for us. We took our places, listened to welcome speeches, the lights dimmed, and a thunderous music started. Suddenly, the first group of dancers, young men dressed in traditional Armenian costumes, came charging onto the stage with such joy, such exuberance, and such an outpouring of love.

That did it. At that moment, the block of ice that had held me prisoner melted, my tears started flowing, actually pouring, and stopped only at the end of the performances, about one and a half hours later.

I was in Armenia.

Seeing those young men and women, dancing traditional folk dances, dressed in impeccably designed and sewn outfits,

I realized that Armenia, lover of art, literature, and music, was rising again, was going to become the culturally beautiful homeland of my dreams. From then on, and every day thereafter, I saw only beauty around me.

Government, business, and housing buildings are made of the *tufa* stone, which comes in various shades of pink, and they are decorated with sculptures. There is a park halfway around the center of Yerevan, and one could see old men working in their gardens throughout the city. Pollution had not reached industrialized proportions. The sky was a beautiful and clear blue. I realized the city of Yerevan was dirty from the dust of constructions, not from litter in the streets.

I had the time of my life talking in Armenian with everyone, even total strangers on the street. I was surprised and very pleased to see a people who are struggling, who are poor for the most part, and yet who exude pride. I found Armenia to have a people who are hardworking, courageous, and at the same time pleasant and welcoming: from the money changers to the cab drivers to the servers in the restaurants to the shopkeepers. In spite of the high unemployment rate, the people were dressed neatly, the men with short hair, the young women in the latest fashionable heels. Everywhere we looked we saw rebirth, construction, gardens. There were flower shops at every corner and the grocery stores were small but clean.

We also visited cities and drove through villages that were

so poor it broke my heart. But I concentrated on the positive—
for the present and for a promising tomorrow. And I touched
Armenia's soil, I ate Lake Sevan's fish, I saw some of the
orchards.

I found in Armenia and its children many of the characteristics
I have in myself. I am strong and look forward to overcoming
the challenges life presents me. I am proud to stand tall at my
four feet, nine inches. I found my best qualities reflected in the
children of Ararat.

Finally, I realized that while I live in the Diaspora, I am no
longer a stepchild of the world. I am of Egypt by birth, I am of
America by choice, I am of Armenia by my ethnic heritage. But
above all, I belong to Earth, just like every other living thing on
this planet.

And in Conclusion

As I look back on my life I can't help but tell myself sometimes, "What if . . ." How would my life have been if I had made different choices? I am sure everyone has those moments of wondering.

What if I had remained in Egypt?

What if I had pursued my dream career of teaching?

What if I had gone to Canada instead of coming to the United States?

Life would certainly have been different. How? I have no idea. I only know one thing: life leads you where you're supposed to be, and wherever you get, you will be at your best. This gives me consolation at times when I am faced with challenges I had not anticipated and I keep going forward.

I wanted to be a mother. I did not become a mother.

I wanted to be a teacher. I only had a taste of it for two years (one year in Cairo and one in Beirut).

But I did fill in those roles in other ways.

I did some babysitting for the children in my family, which gave me tremendous joy. In 1983, my cousin's thirteen-year-old daughter came to live with me for three months while her parents were stationed in El Salvador. I tasted motherhood to a teenager!

During my career, I listened and counseled any of my employees who needed a motherly ear.

As for my teaching career, that came in the package called "supervisor." Training, explaining, guiding, mentoring, were all the details of my job I loved the best and had an abundance of. In the late 1990s, after my retirement from LCP, I started teaching French and English at Berlitz School of Languages in downtown Rochester. I loved every moment of it.

All in all, I consider my life a typical human life, hoping that along the way I touched and influenced in a positive direction many with whom I came in contact.

Who can ask for anything more?

Notes

1. "Frog Legs" originally appeared in *Blue Lyra Review* (2012) Issue 2.2, online and in print. Reprinted here as is.

2. "Diagnosis: Guillain-Barré" originally appeared in *According to Us* (2010). Reprinted here with one minor change.

3. "My Beautiful Alex" originally appeared in *According to Us* (2010). Reprinted here with extensive revision.

Acknowledgments

This dream book became a reality because of the help and encouragement of so many people that I couldn't possibly name everyone. Every time I had a story written which I invariably read to friends and family members, I received positive reaction and this encouraged me to continue writing. I must, however, express my special thanks to Dr. Nancy Avakian, who took the time to read some of my stories and gave me suggestions. My niece Nancy and grandniece Katherine (Katie) were often patient audiences to whom I read my stories and enjoyed their compliments and big smiles. And one of my biggest fans, Cathy Salibian, who encouraged me over and over again.

I must mention my co-authors of *According To Us,* Diane Drechsler and Norma Rappl who were with me along the way, Diane with her total interest and many suggestions, and Norma especially for her long list of possible titles for this book.

Nina Alvarez, my editor, became my friend during the whole process. I will always be grateful for her patience, guidance, and leadership. I learned from her so many phases of the self-publishing process I had never imagined I had to go through.

She was so very helpful in editing my sentences and making them more professional to read.

I want to also mention with pleasure Nina's crew who were involved during the last phases of the production: Carolyn Birrittella with marketing; Raquel Pidal with copyediting.

And many thanks to Kate Turner Jacus who scanned the old and delicate photographs that appear within the book.

In addition, I appreciate the professional work of my friend Millie Sigler who took my author photograph for the back cover.

About the Author

Berdjouhi Esmerian was born in Alexandria, Egypt, in an Armenian home. With world War II disrupting her childhood homes, the Suez Crisis and civil war in Lebanon changing the course of her education, she found peace only when she arrived in the United States at the age of thirty. She spent a fulfilling career at the The Lawyers Co-operative Publishing Company in Rochester, New York, was very active in the small Armenian community in the city. In 2010 she co-authored a memoir anthology, *According to Us*, and has been published in *Blue Lyra Review*.

Made in the USA
Columbia, SC
16 February 2018